LOVE
in the Time of
Impermanence

"This is a beautiful and thought-provoking exposition of the fleeting nature of love and the necessary work on ourselves and in our connections with others that we must maintain for love to thrive and endure."

DR. L. EDUARDO CARDONA-SANCLEMENTE,
AUTHOR OF *AYURVEDA FOR DEPRESSION*

"This is a delicious book. If you don't know what true love is, you will by the time you finish this book. If you're blessed to know love, you will savor every familiar morsel. In either case, the practical meditations will give you the tangible experience of the deep wisdom shared here."

SUZANNE GIESEMANN,
AUTHOR OF *MESSAGES OF HOPE*

"Matt McKay has devoted his life to being a healer of the hurting in his thoughts, words, and deeds. He has walked the talk in his compassionate counseling as a clinical psychologist; and he has talked the walk as a lecturer and prodigious writer. When his son, Jordan, died tragically, Matt had the courage to step through the veil and enter into a cosmological dialogue with his son. In his latest work, *Love in the Time of Impermanence,* he offers the distillation of their joint wisdom in an articulate and comprehensive examination of the origin and motivating force behind all life, namely love. Jordan is proud of you, Matt."

SEÁN ÓLAOIRE, PH.D., COFOUNDER AND
SPIRITUAL DIRECTOR OF COMPANIONS OF THE JOURNEY

LOVE
in the Time of
Impermanence

A Sacred Planet Book

MATTHEW MCKAY, Ph.D.

Park Street Press

Rochester, Vermont

Park Street Press
One Park Street
Rochester, Vermont 05767
www.ParkStPress.com

Text stock is SFI certified

Park Street Press is a division of Inner Traditions International

Sacred Planet Books are curated by Richard Grossinger, Inner Traditions editorial board member and cofounder and former publisher of North Atlantic Books. The Sacred Planet collection, published under the umbrella of the Inner Traditions family of imprints, is comprised of works on the themes of consciousness, cosmology, alternative medicine, dreams, climate, permaculture, alchemy, shamanic studies, oracles, astrology, crystals, hyperobjects, locutions, and subtle bodies.

Cataloging-in-Publication Data for this title is available from the Library of Congress

ISBN 978-1-64411-398-1 (print)
ISBN 978-1-64411-399-8 (ebook)

Printed and bound in the United States by Lake Book Manufacturing, Inc. The text stock is SFI certified. The Sustainable Forestry Initiative® program promotes sustainable forest management.

10 9 8 7 6 5 4 3 2 1

Text design and layout by Virginia Scott Bowman
This book was typeset in Garamond Premier Pro with Gineso used as the display typeface

To send correspondence to the author of this book, mail a first-class letter to the author c/o Inner Traditions • Bear & Company, One Park Street, Rochester, VT 05767, and we will forward the communication, or contact the author directly at **matt@newharbinger.com**.

To the memory of Ralph Metzner,
who taught me how to channel.

And to my wife, Jude,
who every day shows me how to love.

Contents

—◦◦◦—

INTRODUCTION
Love Lives On

Death is the mother of beauty.

WALLACE STEVENS

Everything we know and count on and love is impermanent. That truth crashed down on me in 2008. On an early autumn day that year I learned that my twenty-three-year-old son had died.

Though Jordan was gone, though I could no longer hold him or hear his voice, my love for him remained a living thing. It nourished me and kept me going. It was a blanket that protected me from emptiness and nihilism.

I wondered at love's strength, its unwillingness to die with the body, its resilience in the face of every kind of change and loss this world can throw at us. And I wondered what love actually is, what it's made of. What do we mean, I questioned, when we say we love something? Why, for some, does love die or disappear, while for others even death has no dominion over their love?

As a psychologist and couples therapist for more than forty years, I have witnessed the death of love. Many times. I have seen how emotional pain deadens the will and desire to express love. How it turns caring into anger and contempt. But I have also seen how we can learn to love in the face of monstrous pain and loss. I have learned how some keep love alive in the crushing maw of impermanence.

That is the purpose of this book: to learn to know what love is and how to keep it—even when you hurt, even when things are taken, even as you walk daily in the shadow of uncertainty.

Love in the Time of Impermanence grew from years of seeking and exploration after Jordan's death. But it also came from our living relationship—and from Jordan himself. I learned to talk to him in spirit. For more than a dozen years I have channeled and learned from my son in the afterlife. The books *Seeking Jordan* and *The Luminous Landscape of the Afterlife* are distillations of hundreds of "conversations" between us. The book you are now reading is a collaboration. Jordan's words are offset in boxes and offer the wisdom of a soul who has lived many lives and who understands our fate of love and loss.

We offer this book to you so that whatever changes, whatever is taken or lost, your love will live and be untouched.

1
What Love Is

*L*ove is the most important thing on Earth. It's what all of us seek. We build our families, as best we can, on a foundation of love. Our most valued relationships have love at their core. Our communities, even our countries, are held together with love. And our connection to God, or the Divine, is often described as love itself. Yet for all its power and centrality, love is hard to describe much less define. The *idea* of love seems at once too ephemeral to hold but also too big to corral with language. And when we try to describe it, we are often forced into greeting card clichés because love is conflated with experiences of harmony, romance, sexual pleasure, and joy. Yet love is none of those things.

At its root, love is just one thing. It is relationship itself. It is the connective tissue that binds us together, that creates oneness and belonging. It is a gravitational force that connects you to friends, colleagues, family (blood and genetics don't connect families), a community, a land, and *all there is* (the Divine). And love isn't the emotion or pleasure you take in those connections—love is the connection itself.

All of our core values, the things we hold dear, derive from love—of self, of others, or of the Divine. If you examine what truly matters to you, what your life is about, love is the force behind all of it. For example, all efforts at self-improvement, at personal growth and learning, are motivated by love of self. Everything you do to build and support your relationships is driven by love of others. The work you do and the people your work serves can be a reflection of love. Creativity is an act of love; the appreciation of beauty is an act of love; the great pleasures of the body (athletics, food, music, dance, sexual expression) can all be acts of love. And spirituality—the awareness that we belong to each other and to *all*—is born from love.

We arrive in this world naked and alone, suffering amnesia for our place of origin. What starts to heal that aloneness is love. Love from and for our caregivers; love of a place, of familiar rooms and streets; love of proximate souls whom we are drawn to; love of experiences that bring us joy. The threads connecting us to everything outside of self are made of this same quest for entanglement. Our survival in this difficult place *depends on* seeing and acting on love.

In the same way plants are heliotropic—always moving toward the sun—we are amortropic, orienting always toward attachment and love. This amortropic orientation reflects a basic law of quantum physics: our world does not have separability; objects that have ever interacted are forever entangled. What happens to one soul entangled by love affects the other. Forever. No matter how far apart in space or time they may be. So we are drawn toward each other by love and once entangled, remain so forever. This is the source of all connection.

LOVE'S OPPOSITE

Knowing a thing's opposite can illuminate the thing itself. If the essence of love is connecting, the opposite of love must be the severing of connection. Hate can't be the opposite of love because hate is a form of relationship. There's a painful but deep connection between those who hate one another. Selfishness is sometimes thought to be the opposite of love. But the focus on self doesn't block relationship; it merely distorts it into serving only the self.

The true *opposite* of love is the silence of abandonment, the judgment that says you are cast out, you are not one of us. It is any credo that separates people into good or bad, into tribes where you either belong or you are dangerous and foreign; it is any judgment that dehumanizes and rejects.

The rooms where we feel safe are defined by the familiar, the faces we know.

Everything outside seems dangerous. The people we don't know could do anything, say anything. We protect ourselves by deciding they are evil.

But the mere thought that there is good and evil creates evil. Because it is the means by which we separate ourselves from the other. Reject the other. Dehumanize the other. Separation—the delusion that we are not all one—is what evil is made of.

There is no them. The room that seemed so small that it contained just a single life holds everyone.

Any belief that separates and severs relationship takes us in the opposite direction from love. And any act that disconnects, that breaks the belonging between souls, sets our course away from love. So in love's opposite, we also see love's essence: it is the bond that holds us, that moves us toward the experience of being one.

THE REACH OF LOVE

Because love is relationship, it isn't limited to the connection between souls. We can love objects and places as well as living beings.

The beautiful things that we come to love—whether it's light shimmering in the leaves of an aspen, a cascade pouring between shoulders of granite, or the polished carving of a monk bent in prayer—constitute our relationship to the world. They are physical expressions of the collective consciousness to which we all belong, and our love for them is a mere aspect of our love for *all that is*.

Love can reach to include anything we can see, hear, and feel because love is the energy form connecting the universe.

HOW LOVE EVOLVES

Love is both an orientation and a skill—evolving for each of us personally and also for humankind over thousands of generations. We begin life as self-focused individuals largely unaware of the experience of the *other*. Our own needs and distress are preeminent. But each relationship is a laboratory where we learn more about love. Over time our sense of self expands to include others. What is good for them is good for us; their pain becomes our pain. There is a growing sense of oneness among the souls we connect to, a feeling of belonging, a sense of fates intertwined. Our orientation moves from a focus on *me* to concern for *us*.

Love is also a skill that is forged in the heat of different and often competing needs shown in the face of hurt and misunderstanding and in the slow discovery of who this other really is. These needs are an opportunity to get better at turning love into action and tailoring our expressions of love to what another can feel and receive.

In the same way we personally grow more able to love, our capacity to love evolves as a species. Early on in the development of *Homo sapiens*—as with other primates—we were able to care for partners and children. This caring response could also extend to favored individuals in the clan. Over millennia the ability to love and care began to extend outward—to one's tribe, to groups sharing common rituals and beliefs, to the personification of God or gods, and more recently to humanity as a whole. The history of love in our species has moved from caring for a few nearby individuals to a sense of expanding oneness.

While many of us still experience limits to love—caring mostly for members of our tribe or church or nation—there are growing numbers around the world who feel a belonging to and caring for *all*. This is the trajectory of love for humans—our sense of oneness will continue to deepen and expand until it includes everything that is.

THE FOUR ELEMENTS OF LOVE

Love is active, not passive. It is about what you *do*, not what you feel. And because love is enacted, and therefore a choice, it is something under your control. It's something in your power to keep. Nothing can take love from you—not loss, not rejection, not death—if you act on love every day.

The apparent impermanence of love is an illusion created by the material world. The illusion dissolves every time you act with love. The feelings of love wax and wane. The motivation or desire to be loving waxes and wanes. But the intention to love can be a constant. It is a north star to navigate by; it is the basis for most decision making; it's what guides us through every moment of every relationship.

The four elements, or acts of love, are care, knowledge, compassion, and intention. Each element is a special way we manifest love in relationships. Together they are the fabric that holds everything.

Care

At the heart of love is caring. The welfare of those we love is important; the fate of what we love matters. Caring means we are committed to what's best for the other. We are aware of their needs and react as if those needs are our own. It's as if our sense of self expands to include the loved ones, and whatever happens to them happens to us.

Care is the opposite of wanting. When you want someone—their presence, their attention, their beauty—the focus is on your own needs. You are hungry; you are consuming what you love. Caring moves attention away from yourself. What matters is the other. The beauty of the beloved inspires respect, a reverence, a commitment to protect. Whether your love is for another soul, a beautiful object, or a place on Earth, the commitment is the same: to care.

Knowledge

The adage that love is blind cannot be more false. Love requires us to *see* because if we don't know the other, what is it that we love? Without knowledge, our love is for a fantasy, a projection. The beloved is our own creation, a made-up product of desire.

Love is always active. Knowing what you love involves paying attention—observing with interest and a hunger to understand. In the case of another soul this means noticing how they feel, what they think and believe, how they respond across many situations and challenges, and what they care about. Such knowledge is gathered during the entire length of the relationship. This core activity of love—seeing and learning—never ends.

Loving beautiful objects also involves active knowing. We study every detail of the object; we learn its history. We watch it change as it reflects different qualities of light. We take in what is unique, what sets it apart from every other object of beauty.

Loving a place on Earth requires the same process. We know it in every season, every time of day. We know it close-up as well as in a vista. We know it by touch and sound. We know what harms and nourishes this place. We experience its beauty viscerally as a part of the fabric that makes us who we are.

Compassion

In a physical world everything someday becomes damaged and changed. By time and erosion, by disease, by loss of function, by the endless collisions of cause and effect. Mountains wear away; lakes dry up or become saline; deserts form where grass and trees once grew; whole ecosystems change or die. Everything physical breaks down, the integrity of the original thing worn away and finally lost. Organisms with a nervous system suffer physical pain, and more complex beings suffer emotional pain as well. Love is not love without feeling joined by this fundamental of existence—how we hurt, how things wear away.

This experience of change and loss—the aching sadness we experience at the damage, breaking down, or loss of objects and places we love—causes pain for sentient beings and lies at the core of physical existence. But it is also the source of our compassion for everything that feels. Compassion is knowing and feeling the pain, damage, and loss that touches everything. It is an unavoidable part of caring.

Intention

Intention is the force that turns love into action. It's what expands passive caring into caring behavior; it transforms passive knowledge of the beloved into an active quest to see and understand. It turns compassion into a commitment to hold, to heal, and to repair.

Intention is what makes love real in the world; it is the source of every act, every expression of love. The mother who cuddles and rocks her baby to sleep is turning caring into action—this is the intention to love. A partner who asks questions about how a beloved felt and reacted in a challenging moment is acting on the intention to know. Someone who listens to and validates a friend's distress is turning compassion into action. This, too, is the intention to love.

While the *feeling* of love will come and go, while desire and engagement may change, the intention to love can become a constant that shapes and defines our relationships forever. It is through intention that love never dies.

What connects us to everything is love. Each act of love deepens our belonging—not just to one another, but to *all*. Each act of love strengthens our intention, our very ability to love. So it is the muscle of intention, as it gets stronger, that makes love bloom in us. With each act of love, we grow more able to see, hear, and feel love. Instead of existing in random, isolated moments where its expression is always a surprise, love dwells in us. It becomes our arms that hold, our legs that carry, our voice that comforts. It becomes what we do and finally what we are.

Struggling to choose love, when everything inside and around us clamors to choose relief, is why we're here. What would love have you do? This is the only question that matters, the only choice that we come here to make.

2

What Love Is Not

*I*f love is connection—connection to others, connection to Spirit, and connection to our higher sense of self—then the opposite of love is disconnection, detachment, abandonment, isolation, and severing our connection to others. But between such clearly defined opposites are many experiences we *call* love, or describe as love, but that are not love. Some of the confusion about love is baked into our language (for example, the phrase *I love chocolate*), or grows from hidden cultural assumptions (for example, the idea that falling in love *is* love). The culture- and language-driven misperceptions about love make it important to clarify what love is not.

We also tend to confuse the "doorways" to love with love itself. Pleasure, companionship, sex, and emotional needs, as well as shared values, aspirations, and life-changing experiences can all function as *opportunities* to build love. But love may or may not grow from these gateway experiences. They are not a rationale or proof for love. Love exists only in the connection, not in any of the doorways through which we might enter a relationship.

EXPERIENCES WE LOVE

We use the word *love* to describe many very different experiences. For example, a friend whose first language was not English once remarked,

"You here in America use the word *love* to describe lots of things. You 'love' ice cream. You 'love' your new boots. And you 'love' your wife. It's confusing. What's the difference?" And he was correct. For many of us—no matter what language we speak—understanding the true nature of love can be confusing. One thing seems clear: we often attach the word *love* to experiences that are not describing a true relationship. We can certainly appreciate the pleasure of ice cream or new boots, but these things are merely objects that provide us temporary enjoyment.

When we taste ice cream, there is a biochemical reaction in our mouths and brains that gives us pleasure and reinforces our desire to have more. When we see an object that we find attractive—such as a garment, a piece of jewelry, or even an attractive person—there's a similar biochemical process in our brains that gives us a rush of pleasure and reinforces our desire to see that object or person again. This same biochemical process also happens when we eat chocolate, have sex, or do something exciting like ride a roller coaster or ski down a mountain. We get a rush of excitement in our bodies and we call it love, when really, we're noticing and commenting on a rush of hormones and neurotransmitters that cause pleasurable feelings. This rush of pleasure is temporary. The tendency to confuse pleasure with love is made worse by conventions of language that conflate pleasure (including pleasurable feelings such as sexual arousal) with love.

The problem and potential danger of these experiences that we "love" is that we may have strong expectations that they will last, when in truth they are often fleeting—the ice cream disappears, the boots wear out, or the person you met—with whom you felt such chemistry—disappoints and shows no interest in return.

EMOTIONS AND LOVE

The emotions we call love are a temporary state. Researchers tell us that emotions last an average of seven minutes. Even the overwhelmingly positive feelings we equate with love (such as attraction, gratitude, desire, joy, and appreciation) are usually brief. They arise and disappear, only to arise and disappear again. Unlike emotions, love doesn't come and go—it exists in the relationship itself. If love was merely an emotion, it would die as soon as the emotion ended, blooming and then ceasing to exist with each surge or fall of a particular feeling.

Falling or being in love, for all its beauty and drama, is a temporary state. Over time we habituate even to this most intense emotion. While the *feeling* of being in love may sometimes coexist with an actual love connection, they are not the same. One is limited to the life span of an emotion; the other—once it is rooted in knowledge, care, and compassion—will never end.

Love is what connects, what joins. Always. And so it cannot be emotion because emotions come and go; emotions are ephemeral. Love cannot be a thing such as esteem or respect. These are judgments, products of the mind that change. Love doesn't alter; it can't be lost because opinions or attitudes change. Love is the connection itself, the binding force that joins one soul to another, one soul to all of consciousness.

NEEDS AND DESIRES

Needing isn't loving. The feeling of incompleteness, of having a missing piece that requires some other thing or being, is sometimes interpreted as love. Some cultures have the myth of the "missing half," the presumption that we remain empty and yearning until our other half is found. But a depleted self needing to be filled is hunger, not love. Whereas love is *actively* knowing, caring, and having compassion for another, the person in need often consumes and takes from the other. Love doesn't take. It joins. It holds. It strengthens.

Love is not desire or wanting. It is not seeking joy or pleasure. Desire and seeking are mere aspiration. Love exists in the relationship with what's in front of us. It is the experience of actively knowing and caring for something. Not out of need or desire. Not from a hope for satiety or some happy state.

SELF-SACRIFICE

There are many forms of self-sacrifice. The parent who gives up their own needs and desires in order to care for a child. The soldier who gives up their own life protecting the lives of their comrades, their country. The leader who puts their own life on hold while trying to create a better community for others. And there are countless other examples. In each, a person gives up their own needs as an expression of love for others.

So self-sacrifice can be an act of love, of caring and compassion, a choice born of love, but it is not love itself. Self-sacrifice as a way of life, as the defining aspect of relationship, *is not love*. It diminishes the one who loves; it depletes the soul. Self-sacrifice can be a courageous and loving surrender of self, but it can shape, over time, a life in which your purpose, your personal mission, can be lost.

Love is not sacrifice or unswerving service. Love is not giving up or surrendering the self for another. To the extent you deny and diminish yourself, love diminishes because the *I* has been lost in relationship to *thou*. The loss of self undermines relationship—and love—because love cannot exist between nothing and something.

SEXUAL FIDELITY

Love isn't synonymous with sexual fidelity. Nor, in many cases, is the decision to have other sexual partners a relinquishing of love. Sexual experiences may be an opportunity to express or feel love, but they are not love. They are, at their best, a moment of harmony and union. A window through which, for a brief time, we can see and know each other.

Sexual fidelity is a cultural convention, something that brings safety and trust, while infidelity is experienced as an abrogation of trust and evidence that love is gone. But love is independent of whom we hold and touch intimately. Love is the relationship itself, regardless of desire. Regardless of any moment of physical union. The act of sex should not be mistaken for love.

Love should not be used as a reason to stay in a romantic relationship. So many people cause further unhappiness in their lives by staying in painful relationships because their belief system tells them that they should. For example, in some religious faiths divorce is forbidden or controlled by one of the partners. Others have been raised to believe that once they've made a commitment in a relationship, they should stay, even if it brings great pain or unhappiness.

From a spiritual perspective, each one of us is here on this planet to learn our own lessons. Learning how to love and let go of an unsuccessful or abusive relationship may be a necessary lesson. In relationships dominated by pain, unhappiness, and nonfulfillment, love should never be used as an excuse or reason for further suffering.

❧

Love is not, and does not, depend on a particular form of relationship. If we live together as partners, love does not require us to remain under the same roof. If the relationship includes a sexual connection, love doesn't demand that it continue. If the relationship includes certain rituals, responses, or frequency of contact, all that can change without losing love. The form a relationship takes—for example, the grown child taking care of the aged parent—can undergo the most extreme alteration without the slightest change in love.

This remains true because *love is the relationship*. It is the care, knowledge, compassion, and intention that are the warp and woof of relationship; love is the fabric holding all of us together.

PROTECTION FROM PAIN

Love does not offer protection from pain. That is, having a loving relationship with someone will still not protect either of you from future suffering. All of us will encounter pain—of loneliness, loss, deprivation, failure, feeling invisible, and so on.

Many people equate pain with failure. They think that because they are experiencing discomfort—physically or emotionally—they (or their partner) must be doing something wrong, or not acting out of the highest sense of love or goodness. When in actuality, all things are impermanent, even our pleasure and comfort, even when, as best we can, we are acting on love.

RIGHTEOUSNESS

Throughout the centuries, in every culture, there have been rules established by those in authority about how people should behave and what people were allowed to do. Usually these rules gave control to those in power. Historically, this led to women, children, and minority cultures being targeted, persecuted, and discriminated against. Making this even more unfortunate, many of these rules were disseminated and enforced in the name of love—love of God, love of country, love of king, and so on. Yet in most cases this righteousness—this pretending to know what is morally correct and forcing it on others—created inequalities among many groups of people.

Love is not righteousness and rigid laws. Love supports equality and creates fairness. We are all one on a spiritual level. Like individual leaves that are connected on the same tree, we are all part of the same "One." No individual leaf is more important or worthy than any other individual leaf on the tree, just as no soul or person is any more important than any other. On a spiritual level, love is actually the only "rule."

RELIGIOUS DOCTRINE

Finally, love is not religious doctrine or belief. Sadly, in many cases, imposing religious rules has removed love from people's lives because of the rules' harsh or restrictive nature. Or, worse, there was a threat of removing God's love forever—eternal damnation—if a person refused to follow religious canon. As observed previously, love isn't belief; it is action. It is the act of caring, the commitment to knowing and being compassionate in the face of pain.

God's love cannot be taken away from you or anyone, regardless of what any religious group threatens or says. Love is the reason that we are made incarnate on this planet, in order to learn how to love one another despite the pain and harsh conditions we face. Many people are confused because they've been taught to believe that love is a gift from God, that it's something earned by good behavior. But that is false. Love is all around us, holding us. It isn't a gift contingent on "right" behavior. The truth is, love is a universal constant; it unites everyone and everything.

Love is simple. It is caring for and seeing the other. Love is *doing*, in each moment, what relationship requires.

3

Impermanence and Love

Nothing stays the same in our physical realm. All things change, some things die, others dissolve, and some things disappear forever. From the moment we are conceived in our mother's womb, we are awash in a sea of changes, loss, and impermanence. As we age, our health fluctuates and eventually we (and everyone we know) will die. Our abilities to complete tasks, to do things physically, and to think clearly also may deteriorate. Physically, our bodies change even when we are in the best of health. The cells in our bodies are constantly dying, regenerating, and being replaced. The "you" who exists today is actually different from the "you" you were ten years ago, because every cell in your body is different.

Everything around us changes as well. Riverbeds shift or dry up; mountains erode or crash down in quakes; buildings are erected and collapse; forests are cut, die, or evolve into fields or parking lots; landslides change the shoreline. All that's familiar is eventually replaced.

Emotions come and go too. The happiness you felt several days or weeks ago when something pleasant happened to you waned, perhaps as soon as you went back to work the next day or turned on the evening news that night. Sadness is impermanent as well. Even in cases of clinical depression, we can recognize that subtle shades of other emotions also rise and fall, come and go. Sometimes even pleasant emotions are experienced in between the periods of sadness.

All emotional pain rises, falls, and changes into other feelings, such as regret, anger, sadness, or relief. So, impermanence refers not only to what can be lost (health, a job, a relationship, and so on) but also to the emotional pain that shows up afterward.

Desires, attractions, temptations, wants, longings, tastes, and satiation are also impermanent. The things you wanted most in childhood are likely just humorous memories now that you are an adult. The person or job you were attracted to five years ago might now seem surprising as your tastes and talents have also changed. And even the things that once brought you happiness—the things you felt most attached to in the past—might seem unimportant by comparison to the things that now bring you joy.

Even our judgments change. Our beliefs about good and bad, right and wrong, fair and unfair are often impermanent. They can evolve as we grow older, gain more wisdom, and see the world in various "colors" or "shades of gray," rather than just "black or white."

Impermanence is the natural state of everything in the physical universe—it is all constantly changing and devolving and reforming. So impermanence of matter isn't an illusion. That is the nature of matter and form. Consciousness, however, is eternal. It evolves but is never lost. There is no difference between each individual soul and the Divine. It is only a matter of scale.

What can we truly count on if everything is changing and dissolving within us and around us? If the people we know are all going to be lost, to death or changing circumstances, then why have relationships at all? The answer is love. Love is constant. Love is eternal. And love never dies. If you accept that there is an eternal divine force in the universe (*all*, the whole, collective consciousness), and that we are a part of that eternal divine force, then the Divine, love, and our souls must all be eternal. The purpose of our existence is to learn (and relearn) lessons about love and relationship with others. Impermanence is an essential piece of that learning. The experience of loss or change can provide an opportunity to develop knowledge, insight, and wisdom, not only for each individual but for the collective nature of the Divine as well.

It is natural that we should want good things to remain "forever," whether these good things are happiness, wealth, relationships, or some prized possession. But if things remained the same, there would be less opportunity for the growth and development of our souls. Just as you cannot appreciate the sunshine without darkness, or sweet flavors without bitter tastes, we cannot fully appreciate love without the possibility of change and loss.

The material world forces us to respond to constant change. Through change and loss, we make discoveries about love and are rewarded with profound lessons. We have a lifelong course in the school of impermanence. Amnesia keeps us from seeing through the loss and impermanence to what is eternal—our souls and our connection through love to *all*. If we saw through the impermanence, we wouldn't learn much.

Consider how you might approach your own relationships differently now, acknowledging that they are all impermanent on this material plane of existence. It can be very painful to lose the things we love and to acknowledge that nothing of this world will last forever. But in that lies the true lesson of love: learning to love despite knowing that all things are temporary can make what we love even more valuable, more important. And, in the end, remember that love itself continues, our souls continue, and the divine spirit that unites us all will also continue, with each of us as part of it.

On Earth, impermanence is a gift to each soul and all consciousness. It allows us to experience loss and change and learn the lessons inherent in everything that happens to us. Every choice we make forces a disturbance in the field of cause and effect and changes something. We often experience this change as a threatening force of impermanence, but actually it is the gateway to wisdom.

4

Where Love Starts

*L*ove starts inside you. The ability to love others grows from love of self. It begins with gratitude for life: for a self that can see and hear and feel; for consciousness that can observe and learn; for a mind that can choose; and for a body that can take action. You came here for the privilege to do all these things. Loving yourself means loving and being grateful for this bit of consciousness that gets to feel, choose, and evolve.

Your flaws don't matter. Your mistakes and failures don't matter. They are just moments in your evolution as a soul, necessary and unavoidable, mere experiences to learn from. We get hooked on our flaws because we are hooked on judgment: we reckon that things are good or they are bad, and so we judge our qualities and actions and determine whether our very being is good or bad.

This is the trap of living in a body: you register experience as either pleasure or pain. So the world becomes dichotomous. Things are good (pleasurable, happy) or bad (painful, unhappy). When we feel pain, it's a bad feeling, and by extension we see ourselves as bad.

Consciousness isn't good or bad. It just is. Your soul, your own sliver of consciousness just is—observing, feeling, choosing, and learning. It gets to do that here, in this place and time, so your immortal soul can grow and evolve. When you know this, when your purpose here is clear, good-or-bad judgments fall away. In their place grows love and gratitude for your self, for this precious consciousness that you are.

Good and bad are mere thoughts. They aren't reality. Reality is what we see and do and what happens as a result of our actions. None of it is good or bad. It is just how we learn, how we become. We go on learning forever. We can't help it. It's what we were made to do. You can love yourself and every day of your life because if you are living you are learning, and so you are always doing what you were made to do.

Self-love isn't earned with "good" deeds or accolades and honors. You couldn't create self-love with a lifetime of service and sacrifice. Those choices may bring a deep, spiritual happiness, but that isn't self-love. In contrast, self-love honors your own consciousness and its beautiful, challenging mission to learn and grow. All your pain, all your mistakes, struggles, and failures aren't evidence that you're bad or grounds for self-hate. They are evidence that your soul is doing exactly what it needs to do, which is to grow and evolve. The opposite is also true: your successes and sacrifices aren't evidence of being good. They, too, are just opportunities to learn, just grist for our mission here.

The pain we encounter isn't a misfortune or accident. It is an essential part of life that teaches us how to love.

Self-love can't be given. It isn't a blanket of peace and acceptance that someone provides or draws over you. Loving parents can't give a child self-love. A partner who loves you hasn't the power to germinate your love of self. You know this already. You remember people who grew up in loving families who nonetheless despised themselves. You've seen marriages where a partner, despite being loved, struggles with a deep sense of unworthiness.

Loving yourself is something you can choose to do. It is achieved by authentically seeing and having compassion for yourself. And by actively caring for yourself (more on this later). If you wait to *feel* love for yourself, you could wait a lifetime. The feeling of love—for yourself or others—is ephemeral and fleeting. It happens only in moments when you can see yourself as an attractive, good, or worthy object. A happy collision of events and circumstances can trigger that feeling, but it vanishes as soon as circumstances change. In fact, it can vanish from one moment to the next.

So loving yourself can't depend on emotion. It must be supported by something sturdier, something less contingent on happy events. What about belief? Can the belief that you are a child of God, a soul created by the Divine, create self-love? Not if you grew up *believing* that you were unworthy and bad. Not if you were abused and *believed* the abuse was your fault. Not if you were taught that your only value was serving other, more worthy souls.

The belief that you are worthy of your own love is hard to create. It can't be found in making lists of your good qualities or in the abstract notion that you are a spark of the Divine. No self-esteem program in the world has the power to create self-love when you grew up believing the opposite. Waiting to *believe* in your worthiness is like waiting for the *feeling* of self-love—likely to be long and painful and disappointing.

Self-love can only be found in the daily acts and choices that are the fabric of life. If you choose to act with love—whether toward yourself or others—you become awake to love. Not as a feeling or belief, but as an experience of engagement, of being fully connected. If you don't love yourself, it means you are disengaged—separated—from your own life, from your own soul.

Acting on love creates engagement; *acting on love also creates love.* You act on love toward yourself by:

+ Knowing and being grateful that you are on a mission to learn. Knowing, no matter what pain or happiness you may experience, that the mission continues. It is your work here, the purpose of life.
+ Authentically seeing yourself—as you are—without judgment.
+ Developing compassion for your struggle and pain and knowing how it connects you to every other soul.
+ Having the active, ongoing intention to *care for yourself.*

SELF-LOVE—SEEING YOURSELF

Love is relationship. Love for yourself exists in the relationship, the nexus between the observing you (the you that sees and knows) and the you who lives in the world (the you who feels, chooses, and learns). But your observing self must observe in a special way: without judgment.

Watching without judgment is the doorway to self-love. If you see—without making it good or bad—each emotion, each desire, each conflict, each hurt, each experience of cruelty or kindness, each experience of aloneness or connection, you will begin to know a love of self.

Of great importance is learning to observe your flaws with compassion. This means watching tendencies and habitual choices that negatively impact you and others. It means seeing the unbeautiful in yourself—physically, emotionally, behaviorally—with no judgment. Just noticing what is and allowing it to be there.

Seeing yourself is embracing, with equal measure, the doubt and the certainty, the loss and the connection, the sin and the sacrifice; the fear and the courage. Loving the flaw protects us from being the flaw. Seeing and opening to the pain keeps it from defining us. The more we love the darkness, the more we live in the light.

The pettiness, the anger, the selfishness, and the cruelty must be seen and loved. If these parts of the self are rejected as "not me," they grow to envelope, to *become* the self. The way to the Divine (*all*, the whole) always leads through what is wrong, what we are desperate not to be.

Each thought, each feeling that is rejected or banished, becomes a monster that we feed. We nourish these monsters with fear, disgust, shame, and—most of all—avoidance. The things we fear to think and feel grow large—haunting and powerful—until they seem to become nearly everything that is.

If we reject our flaws, if we label them "bad," they become outsized. They fill the frame of our vision. Instead, they can be just another thing to observe about ourselves. Watching without judgment doesn't mean you fail to notice outcomes, things you do that are effective or ineffective. It doesn't mean you ignore choices and behavior that are misaligned with your values. Paying attention to outcomes—what happens after every choice—is crucial because that's how we grow and evolve. But we can do it without labeling our choices or ourselves "bad."

Attention Meditation

The ability to watch your experience without making it good or bad can be strengthened with something called the Attention Meditation. Here's how you do it:

+ *For thirty seconds observe everything happening inside your body. Notice all sensations as you scan from head to toe. Some may feel pleasant; some may be unpleasant or even painful. Allow each sensation in your body to be what it is without judgment. If a good-or-bad judgment occurs, just notice and let go of it. Then return your attention to your body.*

✦ *For thirty seconds observe your thoughts. Watch them as you would a dog or cat across the room. Notice how your thoughts (just like an animal) move and shift and change direction. Don't try to control or influence them. If a judgmental thought shows up, just keep watching (like you would the dog or cat across the room) and see what happens next.*

✦ *For thirty seconds observe everything outside your body—what you see, hear, and smell. Whatever you may be touching. If a good-or-bad bad judgment occurs, just notice and let it go. Try to experience everything your senses tell you without evaluation.*

✦ *For thirty seconds observe your emotions. Notice if they are pleasant, unpleasant, or neutral. You might visualize this on a meter, where the needle pointing straight up indicates neutral, and goes from painful on the left to positive on the right. Notice where your emotions fall on the meter without judgment. Just allow them to be where they are. If you notice feeling a particular emotion, just name it and practice allowing it without judgment.*

Set your smart phone at intervals throughout the day to do the two-minute Attention Meditation. You are now learning to observe your life without judgment. As you get more practice, you'll find yourself using this skill spontaneously. You can observe every thought, feeling, or sensation that catches your attention—without making it good or bad. And if a judgment happens, you can notice it, let it go, and return to observing your experience.

Seeing without judgment is step one to creating self-love.

SELF-LOVE THROUGH
COMPASSION

Compassion for yourself grows from recognizing your own pain and acknowledging the fear, sadness, losses, and hurts you're facing in this life. There are things you hoped for that never happened and perhaps things you counted on that have been taken.

Compassion for self is a prerequisite for seeing and holding love in the face of change. Since the self is a necessary part of any relationship, compassion for and recognizing the beauty of self is necessary to keep loving others and keep seeing the flame.

Compassion also connects you to the entire human community that at one time or another faces the same pain you do. We all hurt, we all yearn, we all get sick, we all feel the shadow of death. We are together in our vulnerability to suffering.

Compassion is connection to all. No other link between souls on Earth is more profound than knowledge of pain, the shared sense of what it means to suffer.

Briefly scan back over the years, noticing the challenges and hurts, the periods of pain and loss. Notice what you've been through and the struggles that may persist. Now see if you can allow a kind regard for the soul who's faced all of this. It's not pity—feeling sorry for yourself as some kind of victim. This is appreciating what it means to be human—what it's like to live in time and place, in a physical body, on this beautiful and difficult planet.

Self-compassion can extend beyond this moment. It's something you can actively practice every day. The most direct route to self-compassion is through a meditation that helps build an *intention* for happiness and well-being in the face of human struggle.

Self-Compassion Meditation

Close your eyes. Focus on your diaphragm, the source of your breath. Breathe in and allow your belly to expand. Say "in" to yourself as you reach a full breath, then slowly exhale as you say "out," allowing your belly to gently deflate. Keep breathing, focusing on your diaphragm and noting each breath—in . . . out . . . in . . . out.

Inevitably thoughts will arise—memories, worries, judgments. As soon as you notice a thought, return attention to your breath. Just keep noting your breath—in . . . out . . . in . . . out. Always, as thoughts arise, let them go and turn back to your breath.

Continue watching your breath until you feel a slight quieting.

Now bring your awareness inside your body, noting the world of sensation there at this very moment. Touch your hand to your chest. You live in this body. Let yourself be aware of all you can feel. As you hold this awareness, mentally repeat the phrases:

May I be peaceful
May I be safe
May I be healthy
May I be happy and free of suffering

Do this meditation twice daily—in the morning, before the day has begun to unfold, and in the evening, with awareness of all your day has held.

SELF-LOVE— ACTIVELY CARING FOR YOURSELF

Caring for yourself—as an act of self-love—starts with this truth: you matter. Your life and all that you will learn in this life matter. All that you will feel and do matters. All your struggles matter. Every moment or act of love matters.

Because you matter, because your consciousness is unique and precious, you deserve care. Actively. Every day. Each act of self-care builds self-love.

Setting a Morning Intention

Caring for yourself is an intention you can set each morning. There are three components:

+ *How will you strengthen and protect your body and mind today?*
+ *How and where will you seek beauty today?*
+ *How can you act with love today?*

Set an intention to do at least one thing to protect and strengthen your body. It could be exercise, a small physical pleasure, something to release tension, taking care of your health, and so on. Strengthening your mind could include learning something, creative activities, mental games and exercise, closely observing an experience and drawing conclusions about it, and so on.

Each morning, identify one form of beauty to bring into your day. It could be something you see, somewhere you go, something you hear, or something you read. A plan for an evening walk on a tree-lined path, for example, could provide both exercise and beauty.

Finally, each morning, scan ahead to likely events of the day where you might act with love. It could include various encounters with friends or colleagues. It might involve putting love into a task, making sure it's done well and serves others as best you can. It could be showing love to your partner or children. It might be some form of service. There is a paradox here: is it truly self-care to act with love toward others? The answer is another question: When you act with love, how do you feel? How does it affect your well-being? It may be that acting with love is the best way to care for yourself.

Sometimes it's helpful to write down your morning intention as a reminder and commitment to carry through with it during the day. You might make a simple list, like this:

body: _____

mind: _____

*beauty:*_____

love: _____

The central truth of love is that it's an active process. It's something you *do*. Love of self is the same. It's not a feeling or belief. It isn't about being "good." It's the intention to see yourself without judgment, have compassion for your pain, and actively take care of your body, mind, and spirit *every day*.

5

How Loss and Pain
Are Pathways to Love

*A*ll things change. They devolve or take new forms. Our bodies are the chief example. For a while we grow stronger, more physically adept. We welcome these changes because they herald new potentials and abilities. And then the changes begin to accompany a loss of functioning—often with pain and greater limitations—as we age. The body that was strong and held the beauty of youth tires and frays.

Behind these changes is the knowledge—often pushed to the recesses of awareness—that there is an end. That a time will come when the body can no longer hold life, when we must leave this form for something unknown. The body in which we live is the "center that cannot hold" and teaches the essential lesson we face on Earth—how to respond to loss. The losses we face aren't confined to a body subject to aging and illness. All pain is a form of loss. Physical pain, for example, is a loss of well-being. Fear is a loss of safety. Shame is a loss of our perceived worth. Anger grows from losing the expectation that others are fair or just. And sadness grows from losing virtually anything we value. So pain arises from loss, and loss drives the most acute suffering we face on Earth.

All that you love can be lost, and many of the things you love *will* be lost. How do you love knowing that some of what you care for most will be taken? How do you:

+ Relate to a skill or sport you can do now that you won't be able to do later?
+ Relate to creative abilities that you have now but may diminish with time?
+ Love a child who will some day leave you?
+ Love a partner whose personality, attractiveness, and feelings for you will change over time and who could be lost to illness or death before you are?
+ Love friends or family who may leave or have already done so?
+ Continue caring for a place on this Earth that has changed in ways that make it feel different or foreign?
+ Love a thing that can break or be scarred by time?

How does love transcend such impermanence? Must love itself become as transient as the things we hold dear?

CHANGE AS A PATHWAY TO LOVE

The erosions of time and the certainty of change can actually support rather than diminish love. Every possible loss can make what we love more cherished. And every actual loss can make what remains, even if only in memory, more precious.

Everything we love—everything we give care and attention to—changes. And we change too. Our task, and the central lesson of each life, is to see the flame of love no matter what changes, no matter what is lost. Does the old ball player, crippled and no longer able to play, stop loving baseball? Do lovers who have changed and lost much, who can no longer inhabit the same bed, have to give up their love? Or is love a flame that can always be there, that we can choose to look for and find?

We learn to love *knowing* the object of our love can be lost. And we learn to love *knowing* the pain of loss is inevitable.

The inevitability of change can teach us to love more deeply because whatever physical thing we love is momentary. It will cease to be, in some substantial way, the thing it was on the day we discovered it. It will change in our hands, and as it changes we must find a way to love it again. This is our sad and beautiful work on this planet: to see the next loss coming and learn to love what it brings.

Consider how a parent loves a child as it grows. A baby comes into the world helpless and dependent. A parent learns to love how the baby looks, its sounds and mannerisms, and the changes observed over the early months. The baby learns to roll over, crawl, stand, and eventually walk, and each new ability delights the parent. Then the child gets more autonomous, learns to say no, and throws food on the floor. But a parent's love makes room for these new aspects.

The child's personality evolves—they become irritable or sanguine, affectionate or reserved, adventurous or cautious. They are skillful at certain things and not others. They misbehave. Again, a parent's love expands to include and acknowledge each change.

In time the child rebels and finds ways to resist parental authority. There is conflict. The child clings more to friends, and the dependence of the early days is replaced with increasing distance. The child seems to hide and his or her parent may feel abandoned. Eventually, the child goes to college and develops new interests and desires. The child settles somewhere—into relationships and a lifestyle—and calls once a month to say "hi."

The only constant in the parent-child relationship is change. And much of the trajectory of change involves loss—of closeness, of certainty, but also of valued qualities, endearing behaviors, and shared interests that may have disappeared over the years.

In the face of all this change and loss, love usually persists. Wise parents savor every stage of a child's development *knowing* it will soon be gone. And as the next era shows up, they find ways to love and savor that as well. The parent-child relationship is no different from every relationship bound by love. Change is inevitable. Painful losses, hurts, and disappointments *will* happen. Our work is to savor and love what we have each moment. And as the object of our love changes, notice, savor, and love what it has become. We don't just love. We continuously *rediscover* love.

LOVE AND PAIN

So much of what we do and learn in life is about one thing—finding ways to love in the face of pain. Loving without pain is easy, a gift of happy circumstance. It is like the path of moonlight shimmering on a river—a simple moment of beauty. But the loves of daily life are threaded with struggle. Loving in the face of pain is:

+ Comforting a distressed child when you are tired or angry
+ Listening to and acknowledging a partner's distress when you are the source of that unhappiness or when you feel wronged
+ Supporting a friend to do what's best for them when it isn't good for you
+ Giving something when you're sad or discouraged
+ Witnessing and paying attention when you are in physical pain
+ Protecting despite feeling alone or abandoned
+ Saying what is caring or validating despite feeling hurt
+ Acting on love in the face of mistreatment

✦ Acting on love when you are afraid (perhaps of damage or rejection)

These choices show up daily, and in each moment of pain we learn how to love.

There are a hundred ways to manifest love on Earth, and so many of them involve pain and sacrifice (such as healing, holding, protecting, validating, teaching, cleaning, beautifying, giving, joining, witnessing another's pain, caring and supporting in the face of pain, grieving, taking a blow meant for another, paying attention or seeing, surrendering, showing compassion, and many others). Most of these forms teach lessons we could only learn in this painful place. All of them advance the conscious discovery of love.

Pain, in every form and at every moment, offers a simple choice: avoid and run, or do what love asks. As a species, we've developed countless strategies to avoid pain. We numb ourselves with addictions to avoid it. We use anger and blame to avoid it. We withdraw, retreat, and give up trying. We use distraction, excitement, the pursuit of sex, and a host of venal pleasures to avoid it. But in avoiding pain we turn away from love. Love requires action. Action requires effort and a willingness to experience whatever pain or discomfort an act of love might bring. So the intentions to love and at the same time avoid pain don't go together. They are antithetical. You cannot learn to love without learning to have pain.

Pain is the path to love. In the heart of pain and loss is love. By running from pain we run from love. By avoiding pain we lose the pathways to connection. In the heart of pain is a moment when the universe—and our own purpose within it—finally becomes visible. Love and pain cannot be separated on this plane. We learn about one through the other.

PAIN CONNECTS US

Pain not only teaches us about love, it connects us through compassion. It is the common element of our human destiny, and as we recognize each other's suffering we are bonded by it. When we see each other's pain, we know each other's humanity. In our communal experience of suffering is the deepest truth—that we are one, that we are all in this together.

If our great purpose here is to love in the face of pain, then struggling with pain—in every form—must be at the core of our identity as humans. If you want to love another, look at where they hurt. It is when we stare into another's heart, and see both love and pain there, that we know the deep solace of belonging.

LOVE INTO ACTION

To keep love alive in the wake of change and loss requires action. As an example, let's consider a couple—together twenty years and now in their fifties—who face significant physical and emotional changes. He is overweight, gets tired easily, and sleeps fitfully due to stress about his job. She is often away on errands of mercy to help anyone who needs it. A series of urinary tract infections have left her very nervous about germs and health in general. Sex has become uncomfortable because he worries about performance. And for her the man she married is less attractive, and sex now seems associated with infections. He appears preoccupied with problems at work.

She knows he resents her do-gooding and now resists hearing about anyone's health.

A lot has changed for this couple; they now live at a great emotional distance. They'll have to do four things to keep love alive in the face of change and loss: actively care, actively know, actively show compassion, and do all with the intention of love.

The first necessary step is *active caring*. This means being concerned and protective, expressing that it matters what the other feels and experiences. His worries about work matter, as do her concerns about infection. Her commitment to helping people who are ill matters, as does his health and tiredness. Each should now convey loving interest and support—without judgment or at this moment trying to fix anything. The message is simple: I care about what hurts and is important to you. And here's what's crucial: it doesn't matter whether either of them *feels* concerned at the moment they express it. What matters is the *act* of caring, the words and gestures that convey love—felt or not.

The second step is *active knowing*. What does he fear at work? What's his experience when she's gone helping others? Or when he wants to have sex and can't get aroused? What happens to him emotionally when he hears about her health problems? What about her infections has so frightened her? Why is it so meaningful to help others who suffer? What might it feel like if she stayed home more often? What is sex like for her? What is it like for her to listen to his worries?

Active knowing must go beyond understanding a loved one's feelings and experiences as things change. It also includes knowing what they want and how they would like things to be different. What does he need in the way of support or action? What does she wish they could talk about? Such wishes need to be expressed without blame or judgment. They are no one's fault. They are just aspects of what's changed to be seen and understood.

The cornerstone of active knowing is curiosity—wanting to clearly see the beloved. And holding what is learned nondefensively—as a gift, a path back to closeness.

All the changes experienced by this couple are a consequence of long chains of cause and effect. Love allows these changes, seeks for the couple to know each other through them, and opens each to the truth about what the other wants.

The third step is *active compassion*. Knowing each other's pain is the beginning. But mere comprehension of another's pain isn't enough. It is taking what is inside the other inside of oneself. It is—for a moment—holding their pain close enough so it can be felt. It is an act of opening to receive the hurt and humanness of the beloved as something true and important.

Active compassion requires us to describe out loud the pain we see and take in. Once we have listened, gone inside the loved one's skin to feel what's there, then we give it back, cleansed with compassion, so they no longer have to feel alone with their pain.

Our couple can validate what each has struggled with by saying:

- ✦ "I see how the possibility of infection haunts you and brings up a fear of death, and how that makes sex feel dangerous. . . . I see how helping people who are sick gives you purpose and meaning—and how not helping makes you feel empty, like your life isn't important."
- ✦ "I see how in danger you feel at work—like at any moment or for any mistake you could be replaced. . . . I see how hurt and alone you feel when I'm off taking care of people."

The last step is *intention*—the commitment to turn care, knowledge, and compassion into action. It is expressing love not just with words, but with a willingness to do what is good or healing for the other person. As each learns what the other needs—given all that has changed—new choices present themselves:

✦ Is there a way he can soothe or lessen her fear of infection, of death?

✦ How can he validate her fear?

✦ How can sex feel safer, more enjoyable for her?

✦ How can he support her need to care for others?

✦ How can she help with his performance fears?

✦ How could she help him feel less alone?

✦ What could support him when stresses well up at work?

Intention is the cornerstone of love—it is present at the beginning and through every stage of change. With it we can carry love into our last breath.

6

Practices and Meditations to Strengthen Caring

Caring is the expression of love. It's made of two things:

+ The awareness that what we love is special, irreplaceable, and of great value
+ The commitment to act in service to what we love—to do what's needed for that being, place, or thing to thrive, to be beautiful, to grow or evolve, and to however briefly have its place in the universe

Caring is the force that *holds* what we love—not as a form of grasping but as a wish for wellness. Yet caring is more than a wish or desire. Above all it is action. Caring says this to the beloved:

"You are unique; there has never been nor will there ever be another like you—in my life or in the universe. What happens to you matters. Though you will change and your form will eventually be lost, *I will support and protect you.*"

If compassion is the heart of love, caring forms its arms and legs. It is how love manifests, touches, nurtures, heals, lifts up; it is how love persists in the face of change and wearing away.

CARING COMES FROM KNOWING

Caring is an *outcome* of knowing. Light—consciousness—allows us to see and know parts of the world. Truly seeing engenders caring.

Caring reflects a known truth—that this being, object, or place comes from the mind of *all* and is like no other. It exists in a field of specialness and intrinsic worth. Worth and value don't come from being loved. Love and caring arise from the unique beauty and value of everything we come to know. All that we care for is irreplaceable and, therefore, precious. Its existence, its presence in our consciousness, matters deeply. And so it will always be carried inside us.

We live surrounded by beings, places, and things. We move among them, feeling the touch and pressure of their existence. The relationship can be one where care is shown or it can be one of indifference. The light of our consciousness falls where we will it to fall. And where it falls is a choice—to know and love and care for what we see as irreplaceable or to blink and let go.

Meditation on Irreplaceability

This walking meditation (for use either indoors or out) is designed to help you consciously make a choice to act with care or indifference. Record it on your phone and listen as you take a slow walk, observing everything on your path.

Breathe in and let your breath go as you begin to move slowly. There is no hurry because all you need do is look around you. (Pause)

Wherever light touches, love is possible. Notice every place light falls—every face, every branch and leaf, every formation of rock, every animal, every created thing, every shape and plane and contour. (Pause)

Allow the light to teach you—whatever it touches will change, its form will some day be lost. (Pause) Whatever it touches is unique and irreplaceable. It briefly occupies a place in the universe in a way nothing else will. (Pause) It is alone in its special beauty. (Pause)

As you watch where the light falls, let love take the form of caring. Caring for this face, or tree, or rock; this animal or thing because it is special, irreplaceable, impermanent. (Pause) Let it shine in whatever form of beauty it is—even if it is the beauty of decay. (Pause)

Let in gratitude for whatever the light touches, feeling caring and appreciation as the light holds it—in the moment—before you. (Pause)

As you walk, let your eyes fall where they will. Let them surprise you with each thing on your path. (Pause) Everything is special, unique, never exactly this way again. (Pause) Everything matters because it is here. Because you see it. Because you wish it well. (Pause)

Wish everything well that the light touches. (Pause 3 minutes and end meditation)

Practice the meditation on irreplaceability once daily. As noted, you can do it in your house or any other structure, or anywhere outdoors where you're free to walk.

Light teaches us to love and care for the ephemeral, the temporary. Walk in the light. Notice what it teaches. Let it teach you to care for each brief form that love takes.

CARING AS THINGS FALL APART

Care is a psychological (and sometimes physical) blanket that we throw over each beloved thing. It is the will to protect, to preserve as long as possible, to polish the beauty of the thing we love. It is the will to resist decay and dissolution—things falling apart—all the while knowing that decay and reconsolidation to new forms are inevitable.

Care lives inside a dialectic: one must hold and protect the present beautiful form while accepting its impermanence and ultimate loss. Caring is a rearguard action—Sisyphean, really— to preserve what will be taken away.

Think of the doctor trying to heal and save a patient's life. This patient will eventually have a fatal illness. Yet in the meantime the doctor labors to care for a body that is beset with pain and disease. Nothing the doctor does ends death's dominion, but each caring intervention also supports life.

Caring is not something we do in spite of impermanence. We care *because* of impermanence. The forces of dissolution take everything but our own consciousness. Yet we struggle to hold back the wheel of fate because caring and protecting are how love is actualized on this planet.

BUILDING THE MOTIVATION TO CARE

It's not uncommon that we become attached to beings and things without actually caring for them. We take nourishment and pleasure, we take whatever beauty that is there, but we are not committed to service; we give little back. Take a moment to examine the beings, things, and places you love. Make a list. Now put a notation next to the ones where you've engaged in active caring, where you are doing something to protect, support, or help. What on this list do you love but have little time to care for? And of these, are there loved beings or things that you wish more actively to care for? Think about this seriously. Is there a gap between love and action for anyone or anything on your list?

You can generate motivation to be more caring in specific relationships and situations by using the following care-building meditation. Record it on your phone and play it each morning before you start your day.

Care-Building Meditation

Close your eyes and take a breath, letting it out slowly. (Pause) Bring your attention to your diaphragm, the center of your breath. And as you watch your breath, say to yourself, "in," as you breathe in and "out" as you breathe out. (Pause) In . . . and out. (Pause) When thoughts arise, just notice the thought and return your attention to your breath. (Pause one minute)

Now bring someone to mind with whom you have a caring connection. (Pause) Just see them in your mind's eye. (Pause) Recall a moment of caring connection between you from any time in the past. Imagine the scene and see it unfold—what you both are doing and saying to each other. (Pause)

Imagine that person being present to you now. Experience them being here now—communicating in words and perhaps touch the care between you. (Pause)

As you watch this scene, wish them well. Feel your caring energy for them. (Pause) As you commune with them, relax into the loving, caring energy. Let the caring energy enter your heart, your body, your mind. (Pause) Feel the strength of your commitment that they be well and whole. (Pause)

Merge into oneness with this caring energy, your heart open, accepting and taking in this energy. Feel your body and heart unclench and open to hold all the care between you. (Pause)

Let the image of this cared for person fade now. And in its stead allow a picture of someone you will see today. Someone you want to better love and care for. (Pause) Bring your caring energy to this person's face; feel yourself caring for their well-being and wanting the best for them. (Pause)

How can you serve and care for them today? (Pause) How can you help them to thrive, to be beautiful, to grow or evolve, to be all of their potential, to feel loved and valued? (Pause)

Allow yourself to see one caring thing you can do when you encounter them today. (Pause) Commit to it in your heart. You can do this one caring act no matter what happens or gets in the way. (Pause)

Take a breath; again bring the caring energy into your heart. As you let it out you can end the meditation.

CARING HAPPENS NOW

Love and caring happen always in the present. Nothing you've done in the past has any relevance to this moment, to your decision to enact care *now*. The decision to love—to be kind or cruel, to support or go silent, to protect or leave vulnerable, to heal or helplessly shrug—is a decision you make many times each day. There is no escape from the choice. It is our destiny on this planet.

Watch the day unfold. People come and go, entering and leaving the arena of this moment. If you listen, they are telling you about their pain, their need to be cared for, their hope for some small act of understanding or healing. Though they keep secrets, you can know them, hear them, and help that person to move down their path. Every act of caring is sacred because it reminds us that we are *all*.

7
Practices and Meditations to Strengthen Seeing

*L*ove in the absence of knowledge, of truly *seeing* what we embrace, is an act of projection. We literally make up an image of this other and "love" the fantasy. Ideals of beauty, appearance, and behavior are overlaid on a potential object of love. But something is missing—a relationship to what actually is there.

Projection erases the beloved and replaces it with self, with our own preferences and desires. It is Narcissus, enamored of his own reflection in the pool. Authentic love, in contrast to projection, requires open eyes. We study, observe, and learn about the object of our love.

The experience of falling in love is often largely projection in the early days of a relationship. We take a button (certain characteristics of appearance and behavior) and sew a vest onto it (everything we value and desire). As this real human comes gradually into view, we either become disenchanted or learn to see and love who they truly are. This disenchantment is often described as falling out of love, but actually there was no authentic love to begin with.

Quite naturally we all observe the people in our world. Without planning or intention, we remember how they responded across many events and situations, revealing things they said about themselves, facial expressions and tone of voice that gave hints about their inner life, along with bits and pieces of their past that shaped and influenced them. This patchwork knowledge forms the basis of human love. But its randomness—the frequency and circumstances of our observations— also limits love.

Love for another human can grow only on a foundation of knowledge. We begin by seeing characteristic ways of behaving, emotional responses, desires, humor, values—and reach a real but imperfect sense of this soul's essence. The depth of what we know about this other determines the depth of our love.

If deeper love comes from deeper knowledge, by what methods can we move from random observations and impressions to a more profound understanding of this other? A first step is journaling what you know, followed by mindful observation and inquiry.

Journaling What You Know

Structured journaling can strengthen both knowledge and love for someone who matters to you. Here are some of the domains you might make special note of or include in your journal:

- ✦ *Needs: What do they need from life and their relationships? What do they need from you? What do they hunger for? What fulfills them?*
- ✦ *Values: Who do they want to be or become in the world? What do they care about, and what matters most? What are their highest values (honesty, loyalty, learning, creating, caring, and so on)?*
- ✦ *Fears: What scares them? What do they most try to avoid? What are experiences you have shared where they reacted with hiding, withdrawal, or anger? What have they revealed about previous hurts, where they remain vigilant for repeat experiences?*

✦ *Preferences and Sources of Enjoyment: What does this person enjoy? What brings them pleasure? What are their preferred activities?*

✦ *Aversions: What do they dislike and avoid?*

✦ *Abilities and Limitations: What is this person good at? In what arenas do they have skills that help them to function well? In what areas are they less skilled?*

✦ *Emotional Pain: What difficult emotions show up again and again in this person's life? What hurts? In what way does this individual suffer as they deal with life's difficulties and losses?*

✦ *Navigation Principle: How do they make choices (see chapter 13)? How, as they face pain, do they cope or try to move toward what they most value?*

✦ *Worldview and Assumptions: How does this person see their place in the world? How do they view their part in relationships (for example, trusting vs. distrusting; expecting vs. not expecting to be hurt)?*

✦ *Shaping Events from the Past: What happened growing up that created their expectations, their ways of reacting? How have they been treated or loved? Were there traumas or losses that made them vulnerable to pain? In what ways were they hurt that shaped how they respond to pain today?*

✦ *Physical Experience: Does this person experience chronic illness or discomfort? How does their body react to stress and emotion? How much energy or resilience do they have to face challenges?*

✦ *Relationships of Love and Guidance: Who was there for this person—protecting, teaching, pointing the way? What messages did they convey? What did they teach about love?*

✦ *Challenges: What were this person's greatest moments of threat? What goals meant the most to them?*

Complete this journal for one or more important people in your life whom you wish to love more deeply.

Knowing What You Don't Know

During the process of journaling, you'll discover that you know more about certain domains than others. Make special note of the domains where you have little knowledge and wish you knew more. As an example, you might know a good deal about a friend's likes and aversions, but little about shaping experiences in their past or what they fear. The domains you know less about offer an opportunity for deeper understanding—and love.

If you wish to know more, you can set an intention to explore these lesser known domains via mindful observation and inquiry. Mindful observation is nothing more or less than paying attention. If you want to know more about a loved one's needs or struggles with emotional pain, commit to listening when these issues arise. Let your intention to know the beloved become a focus in every exchange, every conversation.

As you learn more, add it to your journal. Continue to update domains. Listen for anything that will increase what you know about the one you love, and record it as part of your commitment to love more deeply.

There's yet another step you can take to learn more about your loved one—inquiry. Inquiry goes beyond waiting for a moment of revelation. It is an active process with directed questions. If, for example, you know little about the domains of values and navigation principle, you might prepare questions to spark some disclosure.

✦ *"I have a sense of what's most important to you, but we've never talked about it. I wonder what seems to matter most right now in your life?"*

✦ *"You've made a lot of decisions in your life. Is there a principle that guides you when you make choices, something that helps you see the best path?"*

As you contemplate making this kind of inquiry, some questions may seem stilted, out of the blue, or even invasive. Work to shape them until they feel more natural, more easily folded into a normal conversation. And remember why you're asking in the first place—to see more so you can love more.

SEEING THE ESSENCE

At some point in your discovery process, you'll need to look past the individual characteristics of the beloved to see their essence, the defining center for this soul.

You have to see a person's essence with the heart, not the mind. This means seeing the whole, the gestalt of the other. The heart doesn't analyze or focus on characteristics; the heart doesn't judge; the heart doesn't like or dislike aspects of the other. The heart sees the essence. The heart sees the beauty and irreplaceability of the other.

Knowing the other, seeing the other, is the spark that inflames love. Seeing the other as parts, or aspects, strengthens the bond. But seeing the center, the wordless sense of wonder at this unique being, shifts love to a spiritual dimension. It is no longer the love of qualities and traits—it is a love of the whole.

Meditation to Open Love of the Essence

The following meditation is brief, yet it can transform how you experience relationship. Over time you can focus this meditation on as many loved ones as you wish. Whenever you want to deepen love—moving beyond particular traits and qualities—embrace the whole of the beloved by closing your eyes and following the simple script below. Recite this meditation into your phone and then do it daily.

Take a breath and let your body release as you let it go. As you breathe in, say to yourself "in" and as you exhale say to yourself, "out." (Pause) Say "in" on the in-breath and "out" on the out-breath. (Pause) As a thought intrudes, just notice the thought and return attention to your breath. (Pause one minute)

As you continue to note the breath in and the breath out, form a mental image of the one you love. (Pause) Hold it as best you can without thought. (Pause) Hold it with no attempt at description or understanding. (Pause) Hold it as both a mystery and something known too deeply for words. (Pause)

Take a breath—breathe in the essence of this other. Then breathe out love to this soul. (Pause thirty seconds) Breathe in the essence; breathe out love. (Pause thirty seconds) Once more, breathe in the essence; breathe out love. (Pause ten seconds) When you are ready, release the breath a final time and end the meditation.

KNOWING THE PLACES AND THINGS THAT YOU LOVE

We can experience love for objects and places because they, just like us, grow from the mind of *all*. We are each thoughts, creations of the Divine, and so are inseparably bound together. The places and objects that inspire your love, while not conscious beings, have nonetheless prompted you to form a relationship. And *relationship is love.*

If you wish to deepen your love relationship to places or things, knowing them is the most direct pathway. This can be done in four ways:

+ Learn more about their origin and history—how they were created or formed
+ Observe them closely in different qualities of light, different seasons, or distances. Observe how they change and how they are affected by time
+ Observe every aspect of their unique beauty
+ Learn how they can be protected or polished in the face of misuse, damage, and time's wearing away

Since they were formed and created in the thought of *all,* objects and places have an essential core that we can learn to see and open to. The more we know—by observing and understanding the inanimate things of our world—the more our love deepens for all that surrounds us.

Your consciousness illuminates all that you look at, every being, place, or thing that you see. You can choose for these to shine with love. Every day you choose to know or not know; every day you choose to see your world or let it gray into indifference.

8

Practices and Meditations to Strengthen Compassion

Compassion is how love responds to pain. Without human suffering there would be no need for compassion, no need to notice and be moved by what happens to others. The Dalai Lama has described compassion as *sensitivity* to suffering within an accompanying *motivation* to alleviate or change it. So compassion is two things: the capacity to observe and be emotionally open to human struggle, and the intention that those who suffer—including ourselves—find peace and well-being.

This doesn't mean deliverance from all pain. It just means finding acceptance and grace in the face of life's painful challenges.

In essence, compassion is knowing that pain is an inevitable and important part of human life and that all who suffer need care and support.

Compassion is love. Seeing the pain of another is love. Caring and having the intention to heal is love. Wishing relief and happiness for others is love.

Noticing Compassion

In order to cultivate compassion we first have to see it in its most common forms—kindness and empathy—expressed by others to ourselves and by ourselves to others. Noticing compassion builds compassion. Noticing compassion strengthens the intention that all who suffer find happiness.

The practice that best supports developing an awareness of compassion is keeping a compassion journal in which you can record daily experiences of received kindness, support, and empathic concern from others. It also should include moments when you performed an act of kindness or experienced empathic concern toward another. This journal isn't about large gifts or great feats of sacrifice and generosity—although such might at times be included. It's simply a place for recognition, at the end of the day, for the kindness and caring given and received. These are small things, mostly, but moments that aggregate into a sense of being a person who can love and be loved. Examples of kindness and empathy might include:

+ *A work friend said, "Glad to see you."*
+ *Someone let you merge into their lane.*
+ *You put a hand on a friend's shoulder and sincerely asked how they were.*
+ *Your sister called and said she loves you.*
+ *A coworker complimented your new logo.*
+ *Someone smiled and held the elevator door.*
+ *You sent a text to a friend just to say hello.*
+ *You called to support a friend going through a divorce.*
+ *Someone smiled and picked up something that you dropped.*

Many days are full of these experiences if you attend closely. Tune yourself to love in the form of kindness; remember and write down each moment. *And as you record each event, notice gratitude—both for what you were given and were able to give. The smallest kindness or moment of empathy can spark, on reflection, a welling of appreciation. Mentally thank whoever gave you that gift or feel grateful for what you were able to give.*

Keep your compassion journal for at least a month. And if you are able, extend this process indefinitely so you can watch how it transforms your sense of self—from lost in your own struggle to awareness of how kindness can connect all of us.

THE COMPASSIONATE SELF

Building compassion requires more than seeing kindness. It means learning to see yourself as compassionate. What is your compassionate body posture: How might you express compassion in your face and eyes, or in your tone of voice, or with your hands? How would you express compassion if you had such a role in a play, if you were acting the part? To become compassion, we may think of it as a character we inhabit, a way we choose to *act*. After a time, the role becomes us, becomes the way we live in this world.

The Compassionate Mind

A good way to enter compassionate mind is through a meditation designed to help you see yourself in the compassionate role. It supports you to embody love in the tenor of your voice, your gestures, the way your body leans toward or away, and the words you choose to validate or to judge. The following compassionate mind meditation, adapted from Paul Gilbert's Compassion-Focused Therapy,* is an important step to allowing your deep feelings of caring and empathy to enter the world. It's suggested that you record the meditation on your phone and listen to it daily for one to two weeks.

---

*Paul Gilbert and Choden, *Mindful Compassion*.

Compassionate Mind Meditation

Take a breath and feel your body start to relax. Bring awareness to the center of your breath, your diaphragm, and just watch the in and out of your breath. (Pause) As thoughts arise, notice them and then return attention to your breath, following a soothing breathing rhythm. (Pause one minute)

Allow a warm and friendly smile to form as your body relaxes more and more deeply. (Pause) Now, as if you were a performer getting ready for a role, form a picture of yourself as you would look at your compassionate best. Recall a moment when you felt strong compassion for another, notice the feelings of kindness and caring and your desire for that person to recover from their pain. (Pause)

Imagine how this feeling of care and kindness would show up in your posture and the way you hold your hands. (Pause) Notice how compassion would show up in your facial expression. (Pause) Note your tone of voice. (Pause) Observe how your body shows your compassion, and how your voice conveys warmth and caring. (Pause) Notice how you feel when you see and hear yourself embodying compassion. (Pause)

While holding your warm smile, imagine how you would speak and move in the world in a compassionate way. (Pause)

While noticing how your body holds and expresses compassion, remember your wish that someone you care about might experience less suffering, or in the face of suffering might still find a way to be happy, to have peace and well-being. See how you might express this wish through your posture, your facial expressions, and your tone of voice. (Pause) Watch how you use your body, your face, and your voice to help someone who suffers feel your compassionate wish. (Pause)

Hold your body in this compassionate pose. (Pause) Notice how your compassion takes the place of blaming or criticizing. Imagine yourself as someone who sees and accepts the pain of others and is aware of pain without judgment, someone who sees what is and wishes for relief, for soothing. (Pause)

Now see yourself from the outside. See your facial expressions and how you move through the world. And see your desire to be kind, caring, and accepting of all who struggle. (Pause) Hear yourself speaking with compassion in your tone. (Pause) Watch yourself relating to others in a compassionate way. (Pause) Now, for a few moments, just watch yourself relating to others as a compassionate person. And see others responding to your compassionate posture, face, and voice. (Pause one minute)

Notice, for a moment, your slow, calm breath, and when you are ready, end the meditation.

While the compassionate mind meditation helps you *see* yourself as an actor in a role behaving as a compassionate person, there is a next step. Now you can begin to develop compassion from the inside through a Buddhist meditation (p. 60)* that supports the deep wish for all to be happy.

The core intention of this practice is learning to develop compassion for the people you dislike as well as like—seeing their pain while wishing healing and well-being. It's important that compassion not be selective, not be reserved for the fortunate souls for whom we care. The human struggle is ubiquitous. It crosses all boundaries. It defines us. It is our citizenship, our proof of belonging here and to each other.

There is no one we can't love because all are in pain, all hunger for relief, all face the uncertainty of sweeping, catastrophic change. Everything we have and everything we know—except our own consciousness—is impermanent and will be lost. How do we face impermanence? How do we go on with life when

---

*Adapted from McKay and Wood, *The New Happiness*.

the papier-mâché elements of our world can break at any time? We go on by seeing we are all captive to the same pain, the same struggle, the same losses, and staking our compassion on every soul who suffers just like us.

As with the compassionate mind meditation, record the following script on your phone, making space for pauses so you can digest the meaning.

Compassion for Others Meditation

Close your eyes and take a breath. Bring your attention to your diaphragm, the center of your life and breath. Say to yourself, "in," on the in-breath and "out" on the out-breath. (Pause) Just keep noting "in" and "out." When a thought intrudes, notice that you've had a thought and return attention to your breath. (Pause) Watch your breath. Notice thoughts, and return to your breath whenever a thought arises. (Pause one minute)

Now place your hand over your heart, feeling the warmth and gentle pressure of your hand. And as you do so, bring to mind a person who makes you smile, who always seems able to bring happiness to your heart. Let yourself feel what it's like to be in that person's presence. (Pause) Now recognize that this human wants to be happy and free of suffering. Just as you do. (Pause) As you hold that awareness, mentally repeat these mantras:

May you be peaceful
May you be safe
May you be healthy
May you be happy and free of suffering

Now bring to mind a person you dislike, with whom you struggle. Remind yourself that this difficult person is facing their own pain and trying to find their own way through life. As they struggle and seek relief, they may also be causing you pain. Mentally repeat:

Just as I want to be peaceful and free of suffering . . .
May you, too, find peace
May you be safe
May you be healthy
May you be happy and free of suffering

Do the Compassion for Others Meditation daily. This practice will connect you to a larger community of souls who are all here facing the epic challenges of life on Earth.

BRIEF COMPASSION MEDITATIONS AND MANTRAS

Compassion lives in the moment, the interface between you and other souls as it occurs right now. To bring compassion into the present moment you can use practices and mantras that evoke compassion almost instantly.

Tonglen for Others

A rapid pathway to compassion, but one that perhaps requires more focus and discipline, is Tonglen meditation. Tonglen is a breath meditation based on the counterintuitive intention to breathe in the pain and suffering of others and breathe out healing love, warmth, and compassion. While the meditation as written here applies to easing one person's suffering, note that you can do this same visualization with several people at a time or even large groups.

Tonglen for others is practiced in this way:

✦ Imagine someone in front of you whom you know to be suffering. See details of their appearance and the ways pain shows up in *their face and posture. As you hold this image, open yourself to their struggle without judgment.*

+ *Now, as you breathe in, imagine you're inhaling this person's suffering in the image of a dark cloud. Breathe this cloud of suffering into your heart, where it softens and loosens any contraction that prevents love. Feel the opening of your heart as all the suffering is transformed there into warmth, compassion, and love.*

+ *Now breathe out healing love, warmth, and the wish for happiness in the form of radiant light. This light is loving kindness. It is your compassionate intention to soften and relieve the other's pain. See them bathed in this healing light.*

+ *Continue with each breath—receiving pain and letting it open your heart while giving out love and light.*

+ *Occasionally, you'll find that something blocks the image of receiving the cloud and giving light. When this occurs, focus only on your breath, saying to yourself, "in" on the in-breath, and "out" on the out-breath. When you feel more calm and centered, return to the Tonglen compassion practice.*

Tonglen for others can be done in as little as two to five minutes. The length of each session is less important than the frequency. This practice will build compassion if you do it twice a day, especially with each meditation focused on the people you struggle most to care for and understand. Eventually, when facing a difficult or struggling person, you can use a Tonglen breath to bring compassion into the moment.

Equalizing Mantra

Equalizing is something you can do at any moment of irritation with or resistance to another soul. It is a pathway to acceptance in the face of disgust or the temptation to reject.

To equalize, first notice your anger and judgment toward the target person or group. Watch the feeling before it solidifies into a fixed mindset. Observe your negative thoughts without taking them seriously—they are just products of your mind.

Now think: Just like me, they want to be happy; they wish not to suffer. Just like me, they are caught up in the drama and flow of life.*

When you pass people on the street, particularly those who seem different or threatening, the equalizing mantra can build a more compassionate relationship. Allow them to walk and talk and be how they are. Then say to yourself: Just like me, they want to be happy; they wish not to suffer. Just like me, these people walking by are caught up in the drama and flow of life. Just like me, they want relief and kindness. Just like me . . .

Eventually you can say the key words, "just like me," to encompass the entire meaning. They are just *like you and this is all that matters. They are human and vulnerable, and at the same time seeking relief and happiness. Everyone you encounter—whoever they are and however they seem—is just like you.*

---

*From Paul Gilbert & Choden, *Mindful Compassion.*

9
Intention and the Moment of Choice

*A*ll significant choices move us toward or away from love. And the most important thing we learn in life is *recognizing* the choices and actions that bring us closer or further from love. Each day is full of moments where such choices take place. These moments are often invisible: we respond automatically, as the choice is out of our awareness. Making these choices conscious—to act on love or not—can be life-changing.

While love is eternal, permanent, the only way to experience that is to turn love into action. Acting on love opens you to Spirit, quiets doubt, and helps you glimpse the connection and belonging that is the birthright of every soul.

MOMENTS OF CHOICE AS OPPORTUNITIES

1. Every human interaction requires decisions about what to say, how to act, your demeanor, and the feelings you convey about the other. All throughout the day you are encountering people, and each of

these moments can be an opportunity to act with love. You see in the examples below that even small expressions of interest or acknowledgment—even to people we don't know—are love. They are choices in a moment of time that express caring and convey awareness that this other person has a life that matters. What they feel matters; their hopes matter; their struggles and pain matter. Sometimes with a single gesture or a few words you can convey all of this. And that is love.

- ✦ Before rushing back to the highway, smiling, making eye contact, and wishing the toll-taker a good day is an act of love.
- ✦ Prior to checking out, sincerely thanking a salesperson for their help is love.
- ✦ Instead of passing by silently, touching your partner's shoulder as you walk into a room is love.
- ✦ Rather than expressing opinions and judgment, asking your son to tell you about his day, then sitting and listening with interest is an act of love.
- ✦ At the end of an exhausting day, reading your daughter a bedtime story is love.
- ✦ Fighting back anger in order to appreciate the circumstances that made someone late is love.
- ✦ Rather than ignoring them, checking in with a coworker who looks distressed is an act of love.
- ✦ Looking glad to see someone is love.
- ✦ Responding to a partner's complaint with interest and curiosity—rather than a counterattack—is love.

2. Everything you do that affects others—now or in the future—can be done with or without love. Usually this means doing a task or a job in such a way that others benefit. Their lives or their environments, even in a small way, are made better. A common theme

of the following examples is that someone, usually not present when the work or task is done, is cared for through the effort. And that the task is done consciously, with service to that person in mind. Consider that:

- ✦ The tile layer who works with precision and careful design is giving love in the form of beauty. Everyone who enters that room receives the gift.
- ✦ The cop who remains watchful, protecting the vulnerable and victims of harm, is acting on love during every moment of his or her vigilance.
- ✦ The gardener who works to make even the smallest patch of lawn or flower bed provide comfort and beauty is giving love.
- ✦ A father who makes a kite for a child—colorful and designed to fly well—is acting with love.
- ✦ A janitor who thinks of those who will use a bathroom, making it fresh and sanitary, is giving love.
- ✦ A flight attendant who is watchful for the needs of each passenger is giving love.
- ✦ A mother who makes a tasty and nutritious lunch for her child is giving love.
- ✦ A school kid who writes an essay that expresses something real or honest is giving love.
- ✦ A warehouseman who loads a truck carefully so no one is hurt and nothing is damaged is acting with love.
- ✦ A volunteer who maintains trails in a much loved regional park acts with love.

3. Whenever you're with someone or something you love, you face a choice—to enact love at that particular moment or not. All interpersonal behavior expresses a valence of attachment from embracing to rejecting. This is not an issue of politeness or socially acceptable

behavior. A *message* is very directly sent by gesture, language, tone, and, of course, our actual behavior. So at every moment, in every important relationship, your behavior expresses the present quality of connection.

+ Slouching and looking away during a conversation conveys disinterest and is somewhere south of neutral on the continuum of embracing or rejecting.
+ Smiling, nodding, touching, or a focused look of concern all push the needle toward an embrace.
+ Validating, expressing authentic concern, and asking questions in a tone of interest rather than judgment all express love.
+ Blaming, judging, turning away, inflicting silence, all convey rejection.

Literally everything we do—consciously or otherwise—tells those we care for whether or not they are loved. And these moments string together into a chain of events that define the relationship, that literally *create* love or its opposite. What you create can be a conscious choice.

Your relationship to your pets and virtually any sentient being works the same way. How you respond when your dog nuzzles you to be petted sends love, indifference, or rejection. And these moments sew together a relationship marked by these same aspects.

There is no escaping this truth: when in the presence of those you care for, everything you do (or don't do) sends a message that shades and colors that time. It becomes forever a time of connection and care, or it becomes something else. So often, without thinking or consciously choosing, we turn moments with loved ones into indifference or even rejection. And those moments remain that way forever. The opportunity to love was lost.

The following brief meditation, used each morning, will set your course for the day:

Focus on your diaphragm, the center of breath and of life. Count each out-breath to ten, then repeat for a second round of ten breaths. Be aware of the day ahead, both its opportunities and challenges. Now repeat to yourself this mantra: Today at every moment of choice, I am love. *Say that slowly, for a minute or two.*

You don't have to plan exactly how you'll respond to each challenge. What's most needed is the intention.

Every moment you are creating yourself. Your life is being shaped. You are creating your relationships; you are shaping them to serve your desires or be containers for love. The meditation above can set your intention for the moment, the day, and with repetition, the course of your entire life.

Wisdom is always connected to action. Knowing leads to doing. Seeing the right path leads to taking the right path.

MOMENTS OF CHOICE AS DANGERS

There are three danger points—also moments of choice—that we must be conscious of to keep enacting love. They are moments when there is strong emotion, moments when there is pain, and moments when we experience strong desires or impulses.

Strong Emotion

Surging emotions almost always suggest the presence of a choice—to act on love versus emotion-driven urges. For example, sadness makes us want to withdraw, anger presses us to attack, and anxiety drives us to avoid, while shame makes us want to hide or attack. But these emotion-fueled urges are rarely aligned with love. They usually drive us to disconnect from others, to wall ourselves off in a world of distress where our primary goal is to protect ourselves at the expense of love and relationship.

Noticing when strong emotions arise is critical to acting on love. If we don't pay attention to surging emotions, we act on autopilot—we are driven to cope and avoid. The intention to love is lost in the compulsion to soothe the emotion—at whatever cost.

Pain

When you are in emotional, mental, or physical pain, choice is usually present, but you may not know it. Pain creates intense urgency to numb or fix or diminish the experience of pain. But these efforts to manage pain often shove us away from love. We numb with drugs, alcohol, or distracting activities and forget about connection. We focus on whatever offers relief while those we love slip down the ladder of what's important to us. Our daily choices are about escaping rather than embracing. As with strong emotions, the intention to love can get lost.

Desires and Impulses

Strong desires usually indicate that a choice is present—whether you see it or not. Desire can motivate you to seek positive experiences or, on the other hand, blindly stride toward something destructive. Sexual desire can, for instance, push you toward bonding, care, and partnership. Or toward exploitation. The desire for any pleasure—from food to entertainment to buying things—is often a moment of choice that can bring you closer or further from love. All strong impulses, particularly those involving leaving or withdrawing (relationships, jobs, places, and so on) can impact love.

Desires and impulses turn the focus toward ourselves and away from others. They cloud our intentions to love and push us into unconscious, automatic behavior. Choice can be lost; love becomes an abstract idea without roots in our actual behavior.

To summarize, strong emotions, pain, and desires are danger zones. They create situations where we make unconscious choices and react without awareness of the consequences for love. These moments, over time, can define our lives and mark our path. In combination, they can deflect us from our mission here: learning to love.

PLANNING LOVE

Since love is action—something we *do* rather than something we believe or feel—we can plan for it. In the same way you map out your day, planning for all the events and tasks, you can plan to act with love. Love is something we do with our hands, with the expression on our face, and with the words formed by our lips. It's behavior: like picking your socks off the floor, like a caress, like nodding or smiling, like any small act of kindness or generosity. Love is listening and repeating back to see if you understood what was heard.

These brief moments aren't big. But they add up to something big: *a relationship made of love.*

Planning to love starts with intention, the commitment to see where love is possible throughout the day. It's certain that you'll miss a lot of these moments because you aren't paying attention or are distracted by something compelling. That's OK. It's the nature of our often frantic lives. But by making a daily intention to love, we open ourselves to noticing more moments of choice, more moments of clarity where the road forks in front of us—toward love or disconnection.

The intention to act on love is not always successful. The message may not be received. But this isn't failure or a reason to give up.

The intention to love is the most important thing. Then you find out whether it works or not. You learn. If it doesn't work, if there are unintended consequences, you have gained wisdom, and the same intention will later lead to different actions and better outcomes.

Those are the two key things: intentions guided by love, and paying attention and learning from outcomes. One without the other may not work.

Morning Intention

The morning intention is a ritual to prepare yourself to recognize opportunities to love. Select a time each morning to do the following:

+ *Take and release several deep breaths. In this moment of calm make a commitment to yourself to notice moments of choice during the day where you can move toward or away from love.*
+ *Formally set the intention to act on love this day.*
+ *Scan ahead to identify encounters and events (with colleagues, family, friends, even strangers) that might offer a chance to respond with love. What might you do or say? How would you convey this intention? See if you can plan three or four intentional acts of love in these moments of choice.*
+ *Briefly meditate on how you experience love by bringing someone to mind whom you love deeply. Notice the flame of this love inside you, even if it's only a brief spark of awareness. Let this moment of love begin your day and inspire choices you make till the day's end.*

Awareness of Present States and the Morning Intention

We explored the three danger zones that can hijack love: strong emotion, pain, and desire. You can begin each morning with a commitment to observe one of these states when it occurs that day. You might think to yourself: Today I'm watching my (emotions, pain, or desires). That's my job, to see the choice each time: emotion-, pain-, or desire-driven behaviors— or love.

During the first week, rotate your morning intention across these three states. Develop the ability to recognize each and see that choice exists before being swept into automatic responses. After the first week, shift your intention to mindfully observe all three states *when they arise: high emotion when it's triggered, pain when it occurs, desire as it drives you toward some impulsive act. As soon as the emotion becomes recognizable, as soon as the pain—in any form—shows up, as soon as desire hits you, commit yourself to see it and be aware that this is your moment of choice.*

Our journey here, and the aloneness our spirits feel in this place, is a necessity for the evolution of love. The trajectory of consciousness on Earth is moving from selfishness (protecting and preserving the life of the individual) to community to oneness. All fueled by *intentional* love.

10
Loving What You Don't Like

*L*ife is full of aversions—things we don't like and would prefer to avoid. There are foods and beverages that just taste bad. There are buildings—ugly, decrepit, or garish—that you'd prefer not to see or enter. Some environments hold beauty while others trigger discomfort or even alienation. You may avoid certain animals because they are unpleasant or threatening. And, of course, there are people you don't like and don't want to be around.

In many cases avoidance is the simplest and best solution. The world is full of people, creatures, and places we can easily do without. But when you are bound in some form of relationship to someone or something that triggers aversion, escape may not be possible or right. How, then, do you love what you do not like?

To begin, it's vital to see liking and not liking for what they are: biochemical reactions. One person finds the smell of roses delicious. Another finds it cloying. Each has a uniquely wired olfactory system that responds differently to stimuli.

Like and attraction are illusions of physical life, of a body and brain that are drawn to pleasure and seek to avoid pain. Liking and not liking are hardwired ways to survive on Earth. But while a bitter taste may warn against eating a poisonous berry, in any relationship aversion obscures the other person. And it obscures love.

If you are in relationship with someone that activates dislike, and yet it's someone important, valued, or intertwined with other people or things that matter in your life, feel encouraged to notice the dislike, but your observation can't end there. Somewhere in that relationship are seeds of love, of knowing and caring. In that relationship, liking and not liking can become less important. Finding a way to love is what matters.

People and things you may not like, but might learn to love, include:

+ your sister-in-law
+ the configuration of your work space
+ your difficult neighbor
+ a threadbare city park
+ an ex-partner with whom you coparent
+ an individual who has hurt or rejected you
+ your daughter's collie
+ your postage-stamp backyard
+ your partner's annoying best friend
+ your son's hyperactive buddy who spends too much time at your house
+ your boss

AVERSION AND PAIN

Examine, for a moment, some of the people and things you dislike. Form a brief image of each. Is there a common factor, something you experience in all of these relationships? Look below your aversion. What happened before the disgust or dislike?

You are likely to find, in nearly every case, that the dislike is preceded by pain of some sort. The person has criticized you, behaves in annoying ways, makes overwhelming demands, doesn't care, and so on. The animal is too loud, too active, scratches the drapes, or just scares you. The thing or place chafes against your sense of beauty, order, and usefulness; or it makes you feel less safe, less peaceful, less content. As these examples show, dislike is rooted in pain, which is usually driven by an aversive experience.

Whatever causes pain, whatever we run from and resist, is just another thing to know, appreciate, and love.

How to Love the Person You Dislike

You don't like a particular person, but you're connected. You wish to be far away, but this relationship is too important to break. This person is, for now, a part of your life. But you have a choice:

+ *You can feel the pain inherent in this relationship, plus the aversion and the need to escape. But since escape is impossible, dangerous, or too costly, you will also feel helpless and stuck.*
+ *Or you can feel the pain that's part of this relationship, but replace aversion and helplessness with love.*

How does this work? Imagine that you are trapped in a room with someone you dislike. They are pacing the perimeter, looking out from each window, searching, picking up objects from tables and putting them down. They are doing what they know how to do in this space.

And what do you do? You can pull as far away as the walls permit. You can look stone-faced, hiding your aversion and pain. You can judge their behavior as bad and tell them how wrong they are. You can get angry. Perhaps you can hide behind something large and protective.

But the pain goes on. Just as you are in this room you are in this relationship. And no matter what you do, that person continues to push across the space, making you feel helpless and controlled by their every action. Is there any way to escape this pain?

Could the relationship change?

To love what you have aversion to, watch it with curiosity and interest. Just observe. Of course, you will have your reaction. The usual pain will show up. Watch that too. In the space between you and the other is a field in which love can grow. In that fertile space is everything you see as well as everything you come to know about the other. In that space is awareness that you and the other are made of the same elements and that you and the other share elements with all that is conscious.

As you take in the needs, the fears, the hopes, and the struggles of the other, they become your own. You begin to recognize these as your own life.

You are one because you breathe the same emotional flame, you seek the same redemption—the same comfort and soothing in the face of pain. You are one because the differences are superficial, unimportant. You are one because you are both apparently alone and exiled to this place. You are one because you have both invented a life in which to seek and learn.

When you see the other and know what joins you, compassion and caring are the *only* outcome. Nothing else can happen.

The path to loving despite aversion is to observe without judgment, without inventing a story of good and bad, simply watching as an astronomer watches the sky. When you observe with the commitment to truly see, there can be no other outcome except love.

LOVING WHAT IS DAMAGED

Everything, whether conscious or inanimate, suffers damage, driven by the endless collisions of cause and effect. The beauty of what is newly formed wears away, becoming the beauty of what has been worn and scratched by time. Everything conscious is changed by the rub and grind of events. And all that change, the way pain etches us, is hard to look at. We tend to run from what has been harmed, what bends and thrashes in the wake of damage.

Damage changes how conscious beings look and behave. The ideal shape and form are lost. Coping behavior develops that is unattractive or even toxic in relationships. Think of a dog with early trauma that runs, cowers, or bites when touched. Think of the person who survived emotional abuse as a child and now reacts with rage to the slightest criticism.

Damage, of course, also affects objects and places. A field with a lovely spreading oak is paved over for parking. Paint peels from the clapboard of a cottage. Fire blackens a forest. The colors of a Rembrandt fade. A Ming vase is dropped. Your grandfather's chair gets wobbly and then cracks. The watch your mother gave you ceases to run. A new, tall building dominates your once beautiful view.

A relationship to what has been damaged is frequently marked by aversion and avoidance. The person, thing, or place seems diminished or ugly. Its function is changed or lost. It acts in ways that are strange or unwelcome.

You can love what is ugly and deformed, what is without apparent beauty. The person with the greatest damage is the most important teacher of love. Loving this person is what heals the juncture of light and dark, allowing you to see what is ugly, what you don't like, with compassion.

Loving what has been damaged—conscious or inanimate—requires active seeing and caring. Seeing means knowing the essence, observing the fundamental truth of this being, place, or thing. What is it here to do or be? How have its wounds or damage changed it, and in what way does its essence—its essential beauty—remain unchanged in the face of damage? Loving what has been bruised by time and loss requires us to see everything—the before and after, the wound and the transformation, the collision with fate and the subsequent adaptation to a new form.

SEEING AND KNOWING
AS A MEANS TOWARD LOVE

Whether it's your hostile sister-in-law, the scorched trees after a fire, your teenage son who rakes you with contempt, the way your bedroom feels empty, or how a lover seems hard and far away, the path back to love always starts with seeing. Knowing your sister-in-law's fear and yearning. Observing the sprouting new life beneath the blackened trunks and branches. Knowing your son's aloneness and his hope to escape the isolation of his family. Knowing the empty feel of a room and allowing in the desire to transform it. Knowing the angry or faraway lover as a lost alien who hasn't yet found home.

The path back to love asks you to see everything. Seeing even the hidden, the angry, and the broken. Seeing even the ugly and unacceptable. Seeing to its core, the existence that keeps bending, bracing for pain and loss, fearing something too difficult to bear.

CARING AS A MEANS TOWARD LOVE

Caring starts with knowing we are joined. Whether we like or dislike the person, place, or thing, we are joined with it. And we can learn to care for it because we belong to *all,* the whole, collective consciousness.

Enacting care starts with recognizing the frailty and damage suffered by the other. They are a reed blown by the storms of time. The form in which they now appear will change and finally cease to exist. Seeing and having compassion for that vulnerability is the first and most essential caring action.

It doesn't matter whether the object of care is conscious. No matter its form, it will change, it will be wounded, and its present form will be destroyed in time. The very fact that everything around us, everything to which we are related, is impermanent and will be lost is our reason to care.

A caring action is an essential response to the vulnerability, wounds, and damage suffered by the other. Caring actions toward another human might include:

- acknowledging pain, loss, or damage
- soothing
- protecting
- empathically joining in their pain
- doing something to diminish the pain or damage
- providing resources and encouragement to strengthen the other
- laughing together at the pain and damage we all suffer
- extracting lessons and wisdom from the pain

Similarly to how we care for sentient beings, we can care for inanimate things. Much as a child holds and cherishes a stuffed animal, you can hold and care for important objects—observing, enjoying, and protecting them.

✦ You can repair the broken watch your mother gave you. Or simply keep it safe, holding and cherishing it at times.

✦ You can care for places you are connected to by repairing or protecting them from damage (joining a nature conservancy, for example) or by enhancing their beauty (painting or redecorating an unattractive room in your home).

✦ You can have an arborist treat or trim a diseased or ugly tree in your backyard.

✦ You might reglue your grandfather's broken chair.

✦ You can clean and reframe a painting you're attached to, and move it to where it won't be further bleached by the sun.

The relationship between your soul and the objects and places in your life is real. You are part of the mind of *all,* you come from the same source. The love for objects and places can be experienced in similar ways to the love of conscious beings.

Take, for example, the sea. Love for the sea can be expressed by *knowing* the many moods of the ocean, observing the effects of weather on the sea, watching ever-changing patterns in the surf, feeling the force and power of the waves, or noticing how light reflects and changes the color of the water. Loving the sea also includes *caring* about the sea—for example, working to protect the sea from warming, acidification, pollution, or depleted oxygen. Even protecting the shoreline and public access can be part of loving the sea.

So love of objects and places can involve similar knowing and caring to what animates the love between conscious beings. Even though an inanimate object can't love you back or actively reciprocate your love, it takes a place in your life and gives you something by the sheer force of its presence—a gift from the mind of *all.*

YOUR MISSION

You've come to this planet to learn how to love in the face of pain. And that includes the aversive people, places, and things that are an unavoidable part of your life. They have a beauty that you must find. They have been hurt and damaged in ways you must come to know. They need acknowledgment, support, or protection. As long as you are in relationship, there is only one choice: to see them deeply and clearly, care for their brokenness, and learn to love what they are.

Our goal on Earth is to see everything and to love everything. And everything we learn to love expands us, makes us more beautiful.

11
Love and Gratitude

*G*ratitude is your soul's healing response to beauty and love. It counterbalances pain—of loss and hurt and the assaults of a physical world on our bodies. There is strong evidence that gratitude reverses the effects of depression and creates both a physical and emotional sense of well-being. It makes us feel centered and whole.

Gratitude cleans the wounds of life. It softens sadness, quiets fear, and helps us survive the blows of injustice. Gratitude heals by moving our attention from all the hurts to what we came here to learn—how to love. And how to see and create beauty—which is a form of love.

Gratitude isn't the swerving path we follow to seek relief from storms. It isn't the moment when the pain recedes, allowing a deep breath. It is, rather, a surrender. An opening to how love lifts us, holds us above drowning ego, above the struggle to survive.

There is an unlimited supply of gratitude inside you. It is created very simply by noticing love and attending to beauty. Gratitude is a well with no bottom that endlessly pours forth healing and relief with no greater effort than noticing the beauty and love that each day brings.

GRATITUDE
AND RELATIONSHIPS

No relationship connected by love is complete without gratitude. It's how we acknowledge each gift. Gratitude arises from the moment you see the other with clarity and deep appreciation and see what the other has given you—how your life has changed and what you've learned.

Gratitude arises from your soul yearning not to be alone. Every relationship that carries some authentic spark of love helps mitigate that aloneness. You carry, almost from the beginning of life, a need to belong. A need to be held with care and attention by others. And a deep and driving need to hold and care for them as well.

Gratitude comes from paying attention to every expression of love that comes to us. And the feeling of gratitude spurs even greater awareness of love. In this way, love begets gratitude, and gratitude creates love.

GRATITUDE AND BEAUTY

Beauty surrounds us. It is the blooms in your garden, a dew-covered spiderweb catching morning light, a child's joyous somersault, the green gloss paint you put on an old pine dresser, a cluster of daffodils, the light exploding through the leaves of a madrone, the final chord of a song, the orange afternoons of autumn, the embrace and movement of partners as they dance, and the color of your favorite shirt.

There is beauty in the way your body carries you, in a smile, in the warmth shared in an embrace, in the design of an old blanket on your bed, in the sound of crickets, the crackling of wood in a fire, or the hard slanting shadows in dusk light. Beauty is everywhere and in every hour.

Seeing beauty, in every form, requires only willingness, a desire to see it, and a commitment to noticing. Feeling the gratitude that arises naturally and inevitably from seeing beauty is no more difficult than paying attention to what is before you *now*.

Gratitude *must* be felt if you pay attention to the beauty that your senses bring. No other feeling is possible, unless it is love, which is likely true because gratitude and love cocreate each other.

GRATITUDE AND PAIN

Pain often blocks the awareness of beauty, love, and the potential for gratitude. Pain puts blinders on us so we see only the hurt, only what's broken, only our own needs. But two things are true:

✦ Even what's broken has beauty. And beauty can often be found in the damage itself: the gnarled tree trunk or the weathered face of a human who's endured much.

✦ We can *choose* to see beauty in a world full of the broken and the lost. We can decide to be *receptors* for beauty, attending to every instance where beauty shows itself. Similarly, we can choose to see expressions of love and belonging, which are constant and all around us, in a world holding so much selfishness and anger.

If we can see beauty and love amidst pain, we can find a way to see gratitude, and if we can find a way to see gratitude through pain, we can see that beauty and love surround us as well.

Even pain itself can be an occasion for gratitude. Pain always teaches, always has a lesson, and can open our consciousness to deep truths. Pain helps us to see love where before it was invisible, see what's important in the moment, and see what must be done to heal or fix something.

Pain is just a moment in time. It, too, is impermanent. It will be replaced by another experience and another. Just as one emotion fades into the next, and one thought slides into another, pain rises, morphs, or disappears in the ever-changing parade of present moments. We can be grateful that the parade of moments continues and that we get to observe and learn from such moments—regardless of their valence on the continuum of pain or pleasure.

GRATITUDE AND LOSS

Gratitude can't be experienced without an interwoven awareness of loss. The love or beauty you find will change or already has changed in ways that evoke disappointment. This being or thing is not quite as it once was, and it will change further, losing one after another of its aspects with time.

Gratitude must always include the painful awareness of impermanence. If you try to stay unknowing of what has or will be lost, if you try to block what has or will inevitably change, you will have little sense of gratitude. Instead of receiving love or beauty in the present moment, you shut them out so the pain of loss can remain unfelt.

Love and beauty create gratitude—but only if you accept that every moment is lost to the next moment, that everything that is will cease to be, that everything you love will diminish and become something else, and that every form of beauty will devolve and be reconstructed by time into another form. Mountains will become seabeds. A beautiful human, beset by gravity, will lose muscle and strength. A moment of limerance will shift into yearning and competing needs. The hand that you hold will become knotted by age. The child you carried and held will become so different as the man or woman who goes out into the world and sends you birthday cards.

This is the nature of time and impermanence. There is no way to let in love and beauty without pain.

Consider this example: Partners who have been together years have carried their canoe to a beautiful river. The light glints from the water, and the pines rise steeply above the banks. They paddle knowing each other's rhythms. They talk of what they see. This is a tradition, something part of the life they share.

But there is pain in this scene as well. They are older, so much more of their lives is behind than ahead. A day will come when they can no longer lift the canoe into the river. A day will come when one leaves the other. And already their youth, their life as parents, their life as builders of career and family has been spent.

They can just be on the river, feeling the pleasant slap of paddle on water, or they can have all of it—the beauty and the love—while allowing all they've been and will be. They can either, in the words of Pink Floyd, be "comfortably numb," or they can intentionally feel everything, including the gratitude to be a witness to this moment.

Every love relationship holds the dialectic of love and disappointment. The disappointment can be poisonous, canceling sometimes the effect of love. Gratitude is the counterweight to disappointment, allowing us to hold love without crucifying the beloved to some ideal. Gratitude softens disappointment into acceptance, into an embrace that holds all.

GRATITUDE AND
THE PRESENT MOMENT

Gratitude always happens now. It's an emotion that's fed exclusively by the present. Gratitude is a long, loving look at reality. You have to pay attention to what's happening right now in order to take it in, in order to see and know and embrace it, in order to feel anything about it.

To feel grateful you also have to *accept* the reality that shows up now. No preferred universe will open the door to gratitude. No wished-for scenario or desire will support gratitude. Only radical acceptance of what is, what you see in front of you, will sufficiently liberate a person from loss and disappointment so that gratitude can rise in their place.

If you are caught in what may happen, or what's already come to pass, this is a barren field in which gratitude can't take root. If you are afraid of or repulsed by the present moment, gratitude can't grow. If you resist seeing or feeling love, gratitude is eclipsed. If a beautiful thing or place sends you into judgment, gratitude won't be found.

So *now* is the only place gratitude can be experienced. Seeing or feeling love and beauty depends on being fully immersed in what surrounds you in this moment.

GRATITUDE
FOR CONSCIOUSNESS

You are a unique creation. There has never been anyone like you before. Nor will there ever be a replica in the future. All you have learned and experienced could only be discovered by you; all your struggles and hurts, the things you decided or tried that resulted in pain, are experiences only you have faced. No one else ever, in the history of the planet, has encountered life exactly as you have.

This means that the light of your particular consciousness, and all that it has experienced, can't be found elsewhere. Without you, the universe is diminished; what you have experienced and learned—no matter how difficult or painful—can't be replicated. So the lamp of your awareness, the watch you keep over everything in your life, cannot be held up by anyone else. The awareness of your role and mission can be the source of gratitude for your own existence.

Consciousness (the Divine, the whole, *all*) divides into parts (individual souls) for this reason: to enter dimensional existence in order to learn about love. The mission never varies; this is why we're here.

The energy we have is given to us by *all*. It is ours to keep, to cherish. Our consciousness is given the gift of sight to take everything in, to receive beauty, love, and pain. This life—each one—is a fathomless exercise in awareness and learning. It is precious because there will never be another life, another string of moments, like it.

PRACTICES LEADING TO GRATITUDE

Gratitude Meditation

It is ideal to start, early in the day, with a gratitude meditation. This can be done in ten minutes or less.

Begin by counting ten exhalations while focusing on the diaphragm— the origin of your breath. As thoughts arise, let them go and return to your breath.

Now begin a sentence in your mind with the words I am grateful for . . . and complete the phrase with whatever form of love or beauty might show up. Look for all the things love gives you. Think of the beauty you've recently experienced or that shows up around you. Notice the things you're able to do or experience that are woven into your current life.

Initially set a timer so you'll have enough time for this meditation. Notice your mood before and after the meditation, and be aware of any change in mood that the meditation might initiate.

Morning Gratitude Intention

As described in chapter 4, a morning intention is the direction you set for your soul during the day. Immediately following your gratitude meditation, set your intention for noticing love and beauty as they occur in the waking hours. By doing this, you are focusing your conscious awareness on these two experiences, elevating them above all else that occurs during the day, and committing to notice every form that love and beauty take during this period.

This commitment is a sacred one—you are promising yourself to be as awake as possible to all the beauty and love a day brings and thus to gratitude. Make the commitment formally by saying these words as the finale to your gratitude meditation: "I will watch, throughout this day, every moment of love and beauty that is given to me."

Evening Gratitude Journal

At the end of the day, after all is said and done, what was given to you by life? Use a special notebook to record each night the moments of love and beauty that emerged since morning. Think of every encounter, every place you went, everything you saw. Run the day past your mind's eye like a video, focusing on every moment of connection and all you witnessed and felt in between. Now write down each encounter and experience you feel grateful for. Keep writing until you've completed a full review, morning to night.

This is a day of your life. It deserves attention. It deserves to be remembered. Every act of love, every beautiful image, sound, or feeling is worthy of gratitude. Journaling these experiences lifts your life above the dark, forgotten moments. It makes it possible to see and recall all the things that mattered, that held love and beauty.

Every week, review your gratitude journal. It will remind you why you came here. Why this life—for all its pain—is worth living.

12
Hope for
Love and Wellness

ope always looks to the future and wonders: Will the things we count on remain as they are? Will things we desire materialize? Will the things we fear remain at bay? Our life, as you know, is uncertain, impermanent. We forever stand on the brink of a future yet to be written. Hope carves the future we want from the truth that anything can happen.

Embedded in our hope is awareness of how little control we often have—of the actions of world leaders, of the economy, of management decisions where we work, of choices made by friends and loved ones that affect us, of our thoughts and emotional reactions, and even what happens in our own bodies. At the center of our hope is awareness that, at best, we can control our own choices and behavior but not much else. This is where phrases like "vain hope," or "dashed hope" come in— they reflect the reality that much of what happens to and around us is out of our control and often turns out so differently from our dreams and wishes.

No one is going to stop hoping for outcomes we can't control. But there is a different, more profoundly trustworthy form of hope that focuses on something we can control: love. Your intention, every day, to act on love and bring it into the world, is something entirely within your power. No loss, no hurt, no emotional or physical catastrophe can take that intention away from you. Even a dying patient, intubated and unable to speak, can convey love with their eyes or a touch. Even if you have lost all financial security, and threats loom, you can still love. If you are scared or sad, you can still love. Even if you have lost a child, you can still love that child and everything the child loved. No matter your circumstances, you can still love everything and everyone that your life touches.

Hope and love intersect in important ways. When we hope for the spirit of love to be inside us and then expressed in the world, hope directly affects our access to Spirit, to love. It opens the door that connects us to each other. And then it reveals opportunities to be loving as they show up in the course of each day.

Hope literally creates love. When you hope for a life and a world with more love, it creates a download of spiritual energy from which each act of love is made. Hoping for love is nothing more than a willingness to access love, to take it in, to let it occupy our consciousness. Hope is the key, hope unlocks, hope says to love, "Come in."

ALL IS WELL

As you know, love doesn't make pain or loss go away. But focusing on love makes life about something other than the fear and avoidance of pain. Pain happens, often with little we can do about it. Accepting rather than resisting unavoidable suffering is the first step to feeling truly *well*. Not well as in an absence of pain or loss but well as in living and acting in alignment with love. This is true wellness and it is not impermanent. It can't be taken away. You can, from now until your last breath, choose to bring love to others and the world.

You are the only one with the power not to let yourself down. That doesn't mean you'll always follow your intention, always act on love. It just means that you have almost no power over anyone else. And if you place hope in yourself, in your own commitment to know, care, and have compassion for others, that's your best chance for wellness. For a life that feels right—aligned with who you want to be and what matters most.

Mantra Meditation for Love and Wellness

The following meditation strengthens the relationship between love and wellness. The simple mantra is the phrase I am love and all is well.*

In preparation for the meditation, consider the phrase I am love and what it means. How do you become love? You are what you do; what you do you become. Each day, in your intention to act on love, you embody love more and more. It inhabits you in the same way a desire or goal can inhabit you. It becomes what you're about, synonymous with your identity and sense of self.

Now think about the phrase all is well. This isn't about feeling well physically. Or about events unfolding as you'd like. It's about experiencing love regardless of the circumstances—feeling personal pain and collective struggles, and yet acknowledging that right next to the suffering is love. It is a sense of peace that you give love and are love. You can see others who do the same. This is what all is well means.

To begin the meditation, focus on your breath, saying to yourself "in" on the in-breath and "out" on the out-breath. If thoughts intrude, gently return attention to your breath. As your mind begins to quiet and you feel a small increase in calm, switch your focus to the mantra: I am love and all is well.

---

*Will Pye, *The Gratitude Prescription*.

Experiment with saying the mantra out loud or silently. Say it at different speeds and cadences. The important thing is listening to the words, I am love and all is well, over and over. After three or four minutes with the mantra, return attention to your breath, noting "in" and "out" for a minute or two more. Do this daily, expanding the time spent with the mantra so the truth of this simple statement takes seed in you.

This meditation presents a paradox: to recognize the assaults and challenges we face and at the same time know—through the love we give and see—that all is well.

Opening to this truth is the purpose of the meditation. Like so many practices, the awareness grows in layers over time. Rather than receive blinding insight, you will gather a sense of the web of care and compassion that holds all of us.

HOW HOPE CAN FAIL US

Hoping for outcomes that serve only ourselves or intensely hoping to avoid pain provides little benefit and almost no impact on events.

Hoping for something that will benefit us alone tends to have little influence on the future. It's when hope is shared across many souls that things change. For example, the shared hope for peace does reduce violence. And the shared hope for love increases the presence of love in our lives.

It's dangerous to hope for things *not* to happen. Visualizing the feared event attracts us to it, and the image may, in subtle ways, begin to affect the cause and effect levers of reality.

Your ego, the ceaseless quest for self-preservation, will continue its job. It will direct your attention to threats and objects of desire. There is no avoiding this. No amount of enlightenment will silence it. The only healthy response to ego, and all it hopes for, is to notice it, acknowledge its urges to protect self, and turn back to your intention to love. Ego will want to send you hither and yon, chasing safety and desire, but it doesn't have to define your life. Ego can become background noise while you pay attention to each opportunity to love.

Think of a ballet dancer whose body hurts and wants to rest. The body wants to move in less uncomfortable ways. It has old, familiar patterns to which it would revert. But there is a commitment, a discipline, and the dancer pushes herself to hold the pose or position long after her body screams to stop.

It is the same with love and the discipline of intention. This is how we direct ourselves to move—even when the body and the ego demand that we do something else.

The antithesis of love is demand and entitlement, which reject love by turning others into consumables, dispensers of the things we want. Love gives. Demand and entitlement extract and manipulate and take.

The hope for having, possessing, or keeping slides into entitlement. The stronger such "hope," the more it becomes an expectation. A hope for love is a commitment to giving and a choice you control. The hope for giving love, for bringing love into the world, can always come true. It can be the one unchanging thing in an ocean of impermanence. The only way this hope can be lost is if we cease our commitment to love, if our life becomes about having, possessing, or keeping.

Hoping to love becomes the intention to love, which becomes each act of love, which becomes Spirit itself.

HOPING FOR
LOVE AND ONENESS

Hoping for the spirit of love changes energy patterns around us. Souls within reach begin to experience a greater sense of oneness, of all being joined. This oneness, this sense of belonging, changes behavior. We reach toward each other rather than take from each other or push each other away.

Love and the sense of oneness are the same thing. In the secular world we love our family and the people we know closely. Beyond that we may come to love people who think like us. We love what is culturally familiar. But love asks that we look beyond what is blood, what's known and familiar. It invites us to look at the pain and hunger that joins one soul to all others.

Oneness means this: that all souls—while separate and individual—are connected and part of a single consciousness. What binds and holds all of us as one is love. Love is the connective tissue, the *entanglement* that holds the universe. The hope and intention to *act* on love each day keeps expanding. In time we belong not just to family and tribe, but to all of consciousness. Spirit.

Hope motivates action. It is the fountainhead of purpose and endeavor. Hope is not only a vision for what you want, but more importantly, what you want to be. Hope is seeing the future you want to create. A future not of things and possessions and circumstances, but a future shaped by love. That future is yours to make—with every choice today and the days after. With every act of love or the abandonment of love. With every embrace.

13
The Navigation Principle

*A*s you know, our lives are a long series of choices, stretching from our earliest responses to family and friends up to our last conscious act. How we make these choices, how we navigate each moment and each challenge, defines our time on this planet.

The human mind doesn't choose arbitrarily; it uses algorithms to predict what will happen in each situation. For example, if your partner tells you they are unhappy, immediately there is a calculus: "If I say nothing, X is likely to happen . . . if I get angry and counterattack, Y may happen . . . if I acknowledge their pain, Z is likely to occur." Embedded in these predictions is how your partner is expected to react, and the emotions you expect to feel in each scenario.

But there is one more element. In addition to our predictions of what will happen and how we'll feel, there is the overarching principle we use to make decisions. This is the navigation principle—how we set our compass, who we want to be in each relationship, and what most matters to us. The navigation principle is particular to each individual and derives from what they think is the most important thing in life.

How we navigate is a combination of attraction and aversion. When we are repulsed by pain, instead of accepting and allowing it, our internal navigation instrument (the brain) is corrupted and makes decisions entirely controlled by which direction, which prospect, is most likely to avoid pain.

When we are overwhelmingly attracted to pleasure, our navigation instrument becomes likewise corrupted, and attention is riveted to the choice or prospect most likely to induce preferred pleasures. When navigation is set on a pleasure course, pain is often unnoticed and unheeded. Pleasure becomes all there is, and we simply don't notice all the pain our choices entail.

Widely used navigation principles include:

+ Steering away from pain at all costs. Stopping or avoiding whatever hurts and doing something else instead.
+ Steering always toward pleasure. Choosing what feels good over everything else, including what's arousing, satiating, or what one desires.
+ Navigating toward power or control.
+ Setting course toward wealth or the gathering of resources.
+ Steering toward the familiar and safe; staying away from change, avoiding the unknown, the unrecognized.
+ Setting course against injustice, toward punishment and revenge. Fighting rather than allowing, surrendering, and letting go.
+ Setting course by ego—whatever enhances the sense of self, of personal value, prestige, and importance.
+ Steering always toward what others want or expect.

Each of these navigation principles creates barrenness. There is an emptiness in seeking what will extinguish or in avoiding the unavoidable, and these attractions can all be lost, with despair and degrees of anguish as a result.

NAVIGATING BY EMOTION OR REASON

Many people rely on their emotions as a guide in decision-making. But it is dangerous to navigate by emotion: away from things that generate fear or toward things that bring excitement. Emotions can offer clues to what is meaningful and loved, but embedded in emotions are drives and urges to act that can take us off course.

Reason can help us accomplish tasks and solve problems. It can tell us why things happen, but it cannot set a course. Reason can't guide us toward what's meaningful and valued or what gives purpose. When the road forks, reason can't show us the direction to head toward love.

NAVIGATING TOWARD LOVE

The only principle of navigation that works is to set course toward love and away from the obsessions with self—pleasure, certainty, safety, resentment, importance, aggrandizement—or the expectations of others.

When you set course toward love, there is nothing to avoid. Pain comes and goes as a lesson, an event of living, rather than an affliction. Pain is merely a by-product of life, and the means by which we learn. Pleasure, too, is a fleeting and unremarkable product of physical life.

There is no path toward love; only intention.

We can navigate by and toward love in a number of ways:

1. We can choose to see the pain and struggle of others and enhance compassion as a path toward love (find compassion meditations in chapter 8).

2. We can use morning intention (p. 71) to notice opportunities for love throughout the day.

3. We can use a specific meditation (p. 68) to recognize the moment of choice. The moment of choice is virtually anything that happens between you and any other soul. The direction life takes depends on how you navigate through each moment of choice. Whether you seek pleasure and avoid pain or remember the intention to love.

4. We can be guided by a sense of what's meaningful, our own particular life purpose that flowers from the root of love.

You have come here to be and do and learn something. That was your reason to be in a place with so many opportunities to suffer. This is the crucible that refines life to its essence—who you will be when you hurt. What you will do when challenged to choose. What you will learn from every choice. This is your mission. And how you navigate depends, in part, on awareness of your unique purpose in this life. The eulogy exercise (explained below) can help clarify life purpose.

Eulogy Exercise

Imagine that you have died, and that someone is delivering your eulogy at your funeral service. Hear the words that summarize what you most cared about in your life, and what you most wanted to be and do. Focus less on what you are now, but rather on what you want to be. Inspire yourself by writing, in a few sentences, the key values that you wish to animate your life. How would you want to be remembered? What is the legacy of all your struggles and choices? Notice how closely your legacy aligns with love.

This is your purpose. This is why you are here. Start each day with awareness of your mission. From this moment of clarity comes every choice, every possible direction that life can take.

Meaningful goals and pursuits are how life purpose expresses itself during particular periods and in specific settings. Examples include:

+ Creating environments of beauty and peace
+ Having and caring for a family
+ Teaching, conveying knowledge
+ Serving the needs of others
+ Creating positive change in one's community
+ Bringing laughter or enjoyment to others
+ Artistic expression of ineffable truths
+ Learning
+ Making something useful
+ Sharing another's burden by being a support
+ Creating an enterprise that offers products or services of value
+ Strengthening one's body or mind

Notice that what's meaningful derives from love. Each meaningful pursuit is a particular expression of love—for others or self.

Navigate toward meaning. You love what is meaningful to you, and everything infused with meaning *creates* love. Meaning is anything that attracts the soul, anything that is the soul's work in a particular life.

We each have different sets of meanings. But they are all rooted in love and service. They are what the soul, undamaged by the drives of ego, will naturally seek. We need only pay attention, and then set course toward what the soul wants, and the tasks—in this life—it has set for itself.

14
Love after Life

*L*ove is the gravitational force that binds together all consciousness and every conscious being. Love never dies. How do we know that? There's a vast literature of channeled communications that shows wide agreement on the nature of love in the afterlife and how it contrasts with forms of love we know on Earth. In our lives here we seek to love in the face of pain, loss, and hurt, despite our drives and desires and all our instincts of self-protection. We hide from each other for fear of being rejected, cast out. We try to love without clearly seeing the other, knowing the other. We seek to care with only a faint impression of the other's pain.

We are desperate not to be alone, but all our tendrils of connection seem thin and vulnerable to severing. Our attachments here must always hold the dialectic of love and disappointment; love and anxiety. These struggles are a natural outcome of life in a physical body and physical world. Love is hard work on this planet.

Our dense physical form on Earth prevents us from merging with each other. So love must be an exchange of something passed between us. Love must be expressed in words and touch that can't penetrate the inviolate boundary of the other. In the afterlife a soul's energy form isn't dense, but spacious.

Souls can be permeable and merge, which allows a much deeper knowing, caring, and accepting than we can achieve on Earth.

LOVE AND DEATH

Love isn't lost when someone dies. It is transformed from words and touch into a telepathic connection. Because the death of a body can't end the consciousness housed within it, death can't sever the ties of love that connect the living and souls on the other side. So death has no dominion over the life of the soul, nor can it diminish the love that holds all of us.

Souls in spirit often elect to stay involved with loved ones who are still incarnate. The strands that connect them are energy conduits through which flow a deep sense of love and belonging.

So our love for the departed isn't lost. Our thoughts and yearnings for them aren't sent to some dead letter box with no reply. On Earth, when we remember the dead, a door opens between worlds. We have the power to connect to that departed soul. They receive every fond thought, every message from the heart. In fact, they are just a thought away and are usually ready to speak to us (unless the lessons we are learning prohibit it).

The love between the living and dead is immutable; it goes on as a guiding presence in our lives and a foundation of support that holds and protects us. The dead are not gone. They remain spiritual allies, brothers in the drama of life, watching over us on both the good and bad days. The only thing that changes with death is the physical expression of love—the smile, the hug, the kiss. And yet all of that, sweet as it is, is just an approximation of love. The love itself is a force that lives between us that we open to and let take us to the heart of the other.

If you wish to open a channel to the afterlife, the process is easy and simple. In most cases loved ones on the other side will speak to you. Channeling loved ones requires no psychic powers, no clairaudient ability, no special knowledge of the spirit world. The main requirement is love because that is the telephone wire through which these conversations will occur. You can find detailed instructions for channeling at the end of this chapter.

LOVE IS ETERNAL BECAUSE
WE ARE ETERNAL

Love is constant; love never dies. That's because we—all souls, all consciousness—are eternal. We are part of an everlasting divine force in the universe, and we come here—in most cases many times—to learn and experience love where there can be so much pain, so many obstacles to love.

When we are born, it is necessary to forget these past experiences from former lifetimes so that we can make new choices about love and learn new lessons. It is, therefore, part of the learning process that our spiritual memory is wiped clean* with each rebirth so that we can learn anew without much prior influence. In his poem, "Ode: Intimations of Immortality from Recollections of Early Childhood," William Wadsworth wrote:

> *Our birth is but a sleep and a forgetting:*
> *The Soul that rises with us, our life's Star,*
> *Hath had elsewhere its setting*
> *And cometh from afar:*
> *Not in entire forgetfulness,*
> *And not in utter nakedness,*
> *But trailing clouds of glory do we come . . .*

---

*Sometimes people remember snippets of past lifetimes and the choices they made—through regression, dreams, and meditation—but these are usually incomplete memories that serve as guideposts and reminders of what we are capable of doing.

The material world forces us to respond to constant change—both with discovery and loss. And rewards us with profound lessons. Each incarnation is a lifelong lesson in the school of impermanence. And with our death comes the remembrance that we and all that we love are eternal.

LOVE IN THE AFTERLIFE

In the afterlife love is experienced without risk of hurt, loss, fear, or hiding. There is no judgment in the world of spirit, no evaluation that someone is good or bad. There are souls in the transition time after death who still cling to old beliefs about right and wrong and see things through a lens of judgment. But this passes before they are released to the general population of the spirit world. It is impossible, therefore, that souls can hurt or reject each other. Each encounter in spirit includes a deep sense of acceptance, care, and respect.

Souls in spirit, to a degree, are transparent. So each can be seen and known at a much deeper level than any relationship on Earth. The experience of being known while simultaneously feeling accepted and loved has breathtaking beauty—something we have hints of on Earth during moments of profound union. The experience of merging adds to the knowledge souls have of each other. Two and sometimes several souls can merge in such a way that their energy fields overlap, allowing them to see each other from the inside. The feeling is a blissful joining, a communion and oneness in love.

In spirit, because of transparency and acceptance, there is no fear or hiding. While souls can "darken the window" at times to achieve a certain privacy, their feelings, thoughts, and awareness are generally accessible to souls around them. When a soul learns something, for example, nearby souls take in this knowledge. Everything inside an individual's consciousness is seen and received with love by surrounding souls.

Finally, in spirit, there is no loss. Each soul has eternal life. And no soul is rejected, ostracized, or set adrift to live unsupported. The fear of aloneness and banishment we know on Earth dates back to the time we lived in small bands and villages—to be cast out in the cold and the dark was to die. In the afterlife, once we are joined in love the relationship, the connection, cannot end.

In spirit, everything we see we know. And everything we know, we love.

Souls in the afterlife understand something we only catch hints of on Earth—there is nothing in the universe or the world of spirit that can't be loved. It was all made of love; it's all held in the gravity of love.

The Atmosphere of Love

Love in the afterlife, between discarnate souls, doesn't flow through energy strands (as it does between the living and the dead). Instead, love is literally the atmosphere of the afterlife. It is analogous to the air we breathe, and it is the medium through which all communication takes place.

The atmosphere of love is experienced in three ways. It has a tactile quality similar to a warm, gentle movement of air. Love is also light. Mystics, mediums, and near-death experiencers have universally described the afterlife as dominated by a powerful, unearthly light. This light is the love of *all,* of the whole, of collective consciousness. Instead of blinding, it is illuminating. It reveals the beauty of consciousness and all it has created. Wherever souls look, the light offers full and exquisite knowledge of what they regard. Finally, love in spirit is experienced as sound. Not music or notes from a scale, but a harmonic, the blended vibrational energy of each conscious entity. These vibrational patterns, like the sound of wind rising and falling in the branches of trees, become the sonic expression of love in the afterlife.

In spirit love is a surrounding light and sound. Souls "breathe" it, move through it, absorb it. In the same way molecules of air vibrate to create the sound of words we hear on Earth, the atmosphere of love in the afterlife carries all communication. It is the medium through which souls connect and know each other.

Merging with All

Merging in spirit goes far beyond the permeable, overlapping energy of individual souls. There is a possibility, taken up by many, for a soul to merge with *all*—the whole of collective consciousness. It is an experience of such overwhelming power that most souls open this channel for only brief periods. It's like a supercharge of electricity conducted through a thin wire. In a while the wire gets hot and the current must turn off. But while the switch is open, the soul downloads the truth of things, the beauty of things. And that knowing creates an energy, a vibrational force. When we merge with *all,* the light and sound become everything—all wisdom, all beauty, the deepest form of connection and love.

Souls who have learned more, who've made more voyages to Earth and acquired wisdom over many lifetimes, can merge for longer periods with *all*. They are able to hold the energy charge for an extended time. But eventually, even these more advanced souls let go. They must take time to digest what they've learned, what they've felt in the cradle of *all*.

Merging is the highest form of love. It takes us from the solitude of our own experience into the shared realm of conscious beings. In this space we are purely ourselves, open and undefended. We absorb everything. We grow by watching.

This is what awaits us on the other side—a place where whatever we are or do is only received with love. There are moments of great resonance in our life on Earth. But it gets better. Love in the afterlife is a constant presence never diminished or lost. It holds and supports us. It is the breath of our life.

CHANNELING LOVED ONES IN THE AFTERLIFE

In order to begin channeled communication, you can take the following steps:

+ Select a place where you feel safe and grounded.
+ Clarify the spiritual address where you plan to send your questions. Focus on the essence of this soul.
+ Select a talisman—an object that represents your connection to this soul. It could be something that belonged to the person or something they gave to you.
+ Use an object for eye fixation. Candles are effective, but you could also use a mandala, a sea-polished stone, an image of a Celtic knot. Anything that draws your eye toward it in focus.
+ Take a breath. As you exhale, form the intention to open the channel. Focus awareness on your diaphragm, the center of your breath. Breathe slowly.
+ On your first out-breath count *one,* with your next out-breath count *two,* and just continue counting until you reach *ten.* Repeat for one or two more cycles of ten breaths.

+ As any thoughts arise, notice but don't dive into the thought. Just let it go and return attention to your breath.

+ Keep your eyes on the object you've chosen to steady your focus. Now imagine an orb of light—the color of the sun—about six inches above your head. Let the orb grow and elongate between your head and the spirit world above you; it expands toward your loved one. The channel is now open.

+ Write your first question. Use anything from a special notebook to a piece of binder paper. Watch the words take shape on the page and stay open to whatever you receive in return.

+ Listen inside your mind for the answer. It may come in a few halting words (often the case in the beginning). Be aware, as you continue, that channeling can have different forms: (1) the *download* with complex ideas you'll have to find words for, (2) the *rush*, a rapid-fire series of words or sentences, or (3) the *telescope*, a few potent words that distill the essence of an idea or answer.

+ Write down whatever comes without judgment. Listen for the voice in your mind as you wait for the next few words or the end of the sentence. Keep writing down whatever comes.

+ When there is a period of silence, write down your next question. Continue the process until feeling you've asked enough.

It is, of course, your choice whether to communicate to loved ones in the afterlife. But they are there, usually willing and waiting to do so. The love remains, bonding you together as it always has, and it is able to telepathically transmit all questions and messages.

15
To Love Everything

Everything is connected. Like threads in a great tapestry, each dyed a particular color and located in a specific place yet woven together to form one image, we are part of the whole. We are part of one thing that includes the animate and inanimate, the living and the dead, what is conscious and unaware. The rocks and streams and high blowing grass, the wolf pack, the great and lesser minds are part of this one thing as well.

As threads in a single tapestry, as part of a whole, we can love every other part. We can feel our belonging to each woven thread, whatever its appearance or location. The genesis for love of everything is paying attention.

Everything can be loved. Whatever we consciously attend to, whatever we truly see will be loved. Love grows from attention. If you pay attention to the street where you live, you will love that street. If you deeply observe the humans gathered at a bus stop, you will love them. If you touch a carving made by a craftsman long ago, you will love the carving and the one who made it. If you stare long enough at the moon or Milky Way, you will love it. If you let your consciousness expand to include every soul on the planet, now or ever, you will love them, and you will feel your kinship, your belonging to this place, and each other.

CULTIVATING A LOVE OF ALL THINGS

Our *self*, that unique combination of awareness and memory—things experienced, things done, things learned—isn't a static boundary. And we are not isolated inside of it. The border around our *self* can expand and contract; it can grow outward to include everything we see or contract until *self* is reduced to aversion or craving.

You can love anything by extending the borders of *self*, making yourself open and permeable, taking everything you see inside while also giving yourself to be part of the other. It is a merging of forms, a surrender to mutual belonging. Everything around you is part of you anyway in the same way that you are part of it.

Mantra for Awareness of Oneness

There are words you can say to yourself to cultivate this experience. As you are observing something or someone, let go of judgment. Just see what is there. Look at how light touches it or how it moves. Try to observe deeply its beauty or essence. Allow it inside by saying to yourself us *or* together *or* One *or some combination of the three words. You can say the word(s) once or as a mantra or chant.*

Recite the word(s) each time you deeply observe someone or something. This is important. Make it a practice to say us, together, One *on every occasion you become truly aware of something or someone else.*

Your consciousness can expand beyond your body. Your consciousness can "hold" the person next to you. It can hold the light that touches everything you can see. It can *be* the light that touches everything on Earth, every star and planet.

Here's how you love everything: You *look,* and you *hold precious* what you see. You *become* what you see by letting your identity, your sense of self, grow to include it.

Expanding yourself to include others, to bring inside everyone and everything you see is a choice, an act of will and intention. It's something you can do to stop feeling alone in the universe. It is also a way of life. The Earth spins with all of us together; the galaxies—hundreds of millions of stars—move together on their prescribed paths. Experiencing life as belonging together, a part of this whole, changes everything. Our existence becomes joining rather than competing, holding rather than resisting, loving rather than judging and rejecting.

In the same way redwoods grow together, trunks and branches joining around the stump of an ancestor, we can grow in our love of everything that stands within the circle of our lives. We can, like these trees, intertwine or perhaps wither. This choice to join in love or disconnect from much that surrounds us is the most fundamental of our existence.

There is a meditation that can strengthen your sense of connectivity. It helps your boundaries to open. The goal is to include all of your experience, all that you see, in what you love. You are encouraged to record what follows on your phone. It's suggested that you do this meditation daily. It will expand the boundaries of self to embrace and take in all that surrounds you.

Love of All Things Meditation

Begin by noticing your breath, focusing on its source, your diaphragm, the center of your body. Notice the in and out, saying "in" on the in-breath and "out" on the out-breath. Just keep saying to yourself "in . . . out." (Pause) If thoughts arise, as they will, just note them and return to your breath. (Pause) Continue saying or thinking "in . . . out . . . in . . . out." (Pause)

Now turn your attention to yourself, who you are and have been, letting your memory glide over the events of your life. Let yourself notice—without dwelling—moments that shaped you. You are special and unique; there is no one like you. Each moment you remember is how you know yourself, how you became the person you are. (Pause)

See yourself as the holder of all these memories . . . say to yourself, "I am." Repeat, "I am," while holding these memories of you. "I am . . . I am . . . I am." (Pause)

Now notice where you are in space and time . . . notice that there may be loved ones near you . . . and now expand to notice the people and places that are part of your life . . . notice the things in your home. . . . (Pause) Notice the places of beauty and the difficult places. (Pause) Notice the people and places where you work or where other activities occur in your daily life. Notice the people you're drawn to and the ones you resist. (Pause)

You can hold all of this in love. I am. Together. One. (Pause)

Expand now to notice places where you've lived and traveled, near and then far. (Pause) Be aware of the people in those places. (Pause) And now the places you've never been, and the people and things in those places. (Pause)

You can hold all of this in love. I am. Together. One. (Pause)

Now see yourself—a single point of light. You are a glowing star, bright with all your knowledge and experience . . . and find around you other stars. (Pause) At first they are very few and far away. But the few stars become many, the light growing, expanding. (Pause)

The distance is nothing as the light becomes all there is—your star and the many becoming one light. (Pause) One light. (Pause)

Love is the light that connects you to everything . . . feel yourself held. At once your self—and all of the light, all of the love. At once the wave and the ocean. The hand and all it has touched. The driver, the road, and the destination. The lover and the beloved. (Pause)

Say to yourself, "I am . . . Together . . . One."

Take a slow, deep breath. And when you're ready, open your eyes and observe your current environment.

You are not alone. This is your chance to discover that.

At once you are yourself and everything you behold. You are both separate and one. From your small spot in the universe you can watch everything, join and know everything, and feel the essence, the nature, and the light of everything. Which is exactly what love is.

Index